The Wood

THE
WOOD

*John
Stewart
Collis*

English Journeys

PENGUIN BOOKS

Published by the Penguin Group
Penguin Books Ltd, 80 Strand, London WC2R ORL, England
Penguin Group (USA) Inc., 375 Hudson Street, New York, New York 10014, USA
Penguin Group (Canada), 90 Eglinton Avenue East, Suite 700, Toronto, Ontario, Canada M4P 2Y3
(a division of Pearson Penguin Canada Inc.)
Penguin Ireland, 25 St Stephen's Green, Dublin 2, Ireland
(a division of Penguin Books Ltd)
Penguin Group (Australia), 250 Camberwell Road, Camberwell, Victoria 3124, Australia
(a division of Pearson Australia Group Pty Ltd)
Penguin Books India Pvt Ltd, 11 Community Centre, Panchsheel Park, New Delhi – 110 017, India
Penguin Group (NZ), 67 Apollo Drive, Rosedale, North Shore 0632, New Zealand
(a division of Pearson New Zealand Ltd)
Penguin Books (South Africa) (Pty) Ltd, 24 Sturdee Avenue, Rosebank, Johannesburg 2196, South Africa

Penguin Books Ltd, Registered Offices: 80 Strand, London WC2R ORL, England

www.penguin.com

This selection from *The Worm Forgives the Plough* published by Vintage 2008
This extract published in Penguin Books 2009

3

Set by Rowland Phototypesetting Ltd, Bury St Edmunds, Suffolk
Printed in England by Clays Ltd, St Ives plc

978-0-141-19080-8

www.greenpenguin.co.uk

1 *The Wood and the Work*

My task was to clear and thin an Ash wood. It was situated between Iwerne Minster and Tarrant Gunville in Dorset, and belonged to Rolf Gardiner of Springhead, amongst other things a Forester of no mean knowledge and activity. My debt of gratitude to him for commissioning me to do this work and to reap its reward, is outside calculation: I can but dedicate these pages to him.

The last time this wood had been touched was eighteen years previously. It was chiefly composed of ash, though it also contained a considerable amount of hazel, and also some spruce, larch, and oak. In addition there was the eighteen years' worth of undergrowth in the shape of privet and bramble and a great deal of the clinging, climbing, throttling ropes of that hangman's noose called honeysuckle. I could not see into the thickness for more than a short distance, nor advance a single yard unimpeded. As for the ash itself, the trees were of all sizes. There were some very fine single ones, now nearly full grown; but often a clump of five or six rose from one stool, interfering with each other.

My job was to introduce the idea of freedom into this tangle – freedom for the ash. Not for all the ash; only for the best, the straightest, never allowing more than one to remain out of any single clump and cutting down even good ones if they were too close to others. Darwin said that in Nature the fittest survive. In fact, he only showed that those survive who do survive. It is only when Nature is acted upon by Man that the best, the fittest survive. When Man acts upon Man the same principle is not applied. The Spartans alone seem to have pruned our species on principle. We do not do so now, for no one can foretell how great a mind or skilful a hand may belong to a fragile body.

Thus I started clearing and thinning the wood, which covered some fourteen acres. I advanced upon the tangle with an axe, a bill-hook, an ordinary hook, a slasher, a saw, and a pole-saw. Though my chief tools were axe and bill-hook, I used each of the other instruments at intervals, rather like a golfer selecting a suitable club for each new occasion. I put my head down (quite literally) and slashed my way through the undergrowth, brushing up the clinging thorn, the entangling and infuriating privet, and hacking down the honeysuckle's parasitic climbers until I had free play to deal with the trees themselves. Some of them were in very poor shape and it was a relief to get rid of them. But there were many good ones which I had to take down only because they were too close to one another. This sort of thing goes against the grain even when singling mangolds, and in the case of trees it is hard to realize how much room a single tree eventually demands if it is to be a fine specimen. Yet it is a fact that in the first stage of a plantation as many as fifty to a hundred plants may occupy the space taken up in the end by a single mature tree.

The beauty of this job lay from the beginning in the fact that there was so much to show for it. In quite a short time I had made a distinct impression, a definite clearing – the jumble of brambles and shrubs and misshapen trees had vanished from the space I had worked upon, and now just a few straight ash trees stood up clear and free. People speak of 'not being able to see the wood for the trees'. This phrase actually does mean something – (though it might quite easily mean nothing and yet be repeated twice daily by our publicists). It means that a too careful dwelling upon many particulars blinds us from a vision of the whole: you cannot catch sight of the wood as a totality if entangled in the trees. Many botanists are in this unfortunate position. But often the opposite of this is meant. The man who mechanically trots out the phrase that he cannot see the wood for the trees, often means that the confused bulk and muddle of facts confronting him make it impossible to see where his own particular problem stands. He cannot see the trees for the wood. Now that I had already made a beginning, a neat clearing in the wood, I could for the first time see the individual trees.

And as I made a clearing in the wood so also I made a clearing in my mind with regard to timber. As I began to bestow order and tidy up the confusion in front of me, so I began to sort out my odd bits of knowledge about forestry. That is generally my method of advance in matters of this kind. I cannot see, I cannot actualize for myself any department of work unless I have taken part in it myself. I do not possess the politician's and the sociologist's imagination to grasp the actuality without participation. I have to get in touch with it first through work. For me it is first the tool, then the book. I could not take down the word Forestry from its hiding-place in my head and relate it to the world I know.

My first question was naturally very relevant to the work in hand – What is ash used for by man? The answer is that it supplied the material for most of the instruments of husbandry. Perhaps slightly less so now than formerly. An early nineteenth-century farmer declared, 'We could not well have a wagon, a cart, a coach, a wheelbarrow, a plough, a harrow, a spade, an axe or a hammer if we had no *ash*. It gives us poles for our hops; hurdle gates wherewith to pen in our sheep; and hoops for our washing tubs.' Today neither harrows nor ploughs owe much to wood, but we still need it for the other things.

So already an ash ceased to be 'only' an ash tree in my eyes. And henceforth, when I look across any wood like this I shall see more than trees, I shall see their translation into the familiar objects of the farm and the garden. I shall also see tennis-rackets, golf-sticks, and cricket-bats. Above all – walking-sticks. During some days I had a craze for making walking-sticks myself. The method was so pleasant. Having cut down a tree and observing that it possessed some nice straight branches not too thick for a walking-stick, I cut one off just above the junction of a tributary branch and then cut off the latter a few inches below the terminus. That gave me my handle. Then I measured the stick in my hand against my thigh and made a final cut at the bottom according to my needs – and there was my stick. When I had finished off with a penknife I often had an excellent stick.

2 *The Floor of Flowers*

Apart from any utilitarian considerations, I have always been particularly attracted by the ash whose witch-like fingers with black nails claw the winter sky, and by the aristocratic manner in which the leaves are the last to come and the first to go. The larch, the sycamore, and the horse-chestnut will be in rich leaf without the slightest sign from the ash; the maple, the whitebeam, the hazel, and even the elm, the beech, and the oak are often well away while still the ash remains quite bare as if there were nothing doing this year.

An eighteenth-century forester named Gilpin called the ash 'the Venus of the Woods'. Few would subscribe to this if we think in terms of leaves, since it cannot compare with the glories of the beech or the chestnut; but if we are thinking of a naked winter tree then the ash may well claim to be the Venus of the woods. Its branches are at the top of the tree – a crown – in marked contrast with the oak or the chestnut. Thus you can see a long way into an ash plantation and be fascinated by the beauty of the barks. This lack of low branches and late arrival of leaves provided a further advantage for me – a very important one. I could work in the sun till well into May. Furthermore, the amount of light which ash trees let into a wood promotes a fine floor of flowers. How vastly different is the other extreme! – a pinewood floor. I used to take a walk occasionally to a little pine wood a short distance away, and look into its daily darkness where nothing grew and no bird sang. In my ash wood the common wild flowers were abundant. They arrived punctually according to the well-known schedule. First the primroses in March – when I began work. Then the violets, soon to be overtaken by the anemones who in turn gave way to the bluebells, while the ground-ivy and bugle also appeared; though dog's mercury provided almost the main floor of the entire wood.

We call wild flowers common because of their quantity. But this is just where we strike the great difference between the productions of Nature and the productions of Man. When we produce many samples of the same thing they are of poor quality and we speak of them as mass-produced. The mass productions of Nature do not fail at all in terms of quality. Take the bluebell. There indeed is quantity. Yet every single year we are freshly struck by their quality. Only a flower-snob could fail to see that any one of those bells on the uplifted belfry is as delicate a construction as any tulip or any rose. I will not say more beautiful, or less, for in this realm of flowers we actually are in the presence of abundant examples of – *perfection*. I think that perfection is the key to the emotion that flowers cause in us. When a thing is perfect the problem of its existence is solved. Gazing at flowers in a wood an unexpected signal seems to go up; we feel a movement of happiness and hope about everything, there is a suggestion that all is really well, all is right with the world, regardless of the geographical situation of the Deity. It is because of this that all men, even ruffians, feel attracted to flowers. For they do intimate to us that, in spite of everything, all is well. Undoubtedly that is what they 'say' to us, and why it cheers us up to look at them. Philosophers say that all the ultimate problems – freedom, immortality, beauty, development – are presented and solved in plants. 'The flora does not only raise, but also answers, all the problems which the human spirit may propound,' said Count Keyserling. 'For anyone who could understand plants perfectly, life would no longer hold any secrets. And the plants surrender themselves so ingenuously to man. No being could be more sincere than they are, more truthful, more genuine. They perhaps of all the world's creatures represent themselves precisely as they are . . . these blessed, pure creatures are never subject to evil moods, and always mirror the very core of their beings.'

Maybe it was because of this that the Sage who sat under the Bo-tree wanted to make plants of men: and we must admit that a Buddha resembles a plant more than anything else. Certainly flowers inspire us: they hold up before us the image of the Ideal. What we would be, could we be true, they are. Ripeness is all. We know that. We see it in the flowers, they are the mirror in which is glassed that goal. But our greatest problem is our unfolding: in nearly every case something goes wrong at one stage or another. We fall. There is no fall of flowers.

3 The Tree-shed and the Tools

Every day before I went home I put my tools away in my shed. It had been built for me solely by Nature. I discovered a fairly full-grown ash tree whose trunk was hollow inside at the base for about four feet upwards. There was an opening large enough for me to put my tools through it. Here I placed them every evening, knowing they would remain dry and quite safe since it would be hard to imagine a better camouflage for a tool-house.

In spite of being rotten inside, this tree was in fairly good condition. A tree is not useful to man, of course, as timber, if internally decayed either by disease or the tooth of time; but its own health is not affected if the outer sheaths of the trunk are all right, because the life of a tree resides in and receives reinforcement at its circumference and not its centre. Thus many an Old Village Tree while presenting a magnificent foliage in summer, also provides a huge hollow at the base of its trunk, equally fit as a shelter from storms or a tryst for lovers. Once I saw Mount Etna in full volcanic eruption. It was a sight which held my attention. But at the bottom of the mountain there was another manifestation almost as fascinating – the Chestnut Tree of the Hundred Horses which is said to be the largest tree in the world. Thirty men holding hands do not quite succeed in surrounding it, while a hundred horsemen can find ample room beneath its foliage, as indeed was actually proved when Joan, Queen of Aragon, was caught in a storm nearby and took shelter there with her enormous retinue. And at the bottom of this tree a hole runs straight through, wide enough to admit two carriages abreast. It still yields a good crop of chestnuts.

On my arrival in the wood I took out what tools I needed for the day from this tree-shed of mine. Very often I contented myself simply with the axe and the bill-hook. These are two delightful instruments. There are not many agricultural implements one would speak of in such terms – certainly not of the hoe or the saw. But all good men love an axe; and all Prime Ministers and Literary Prophets in their old age are discovered by the visitor using an axe in the garden. Tolstoy regarded axe-work as a religious discipline. Bernard Shaw declares that it keeps him sane. And it was the axe that inspired Gladstone to say to the messenger who came with the news of his recall to office – 'My mission is to solve the Irish Problem.'

I do not know whether there is any absolutely official method of handling the axe. I have no doubt that my own methods leave room for improvement, but I think I must have done the obvious things since in the end my results were good. In cutting down a tree you need to cut low on the stool and to cut clean. A battered, slashed-up stump not only looks unsightly but promotes arboreal disease. Experience taught me to strike down and then strike up, never horizontal, thus carving out a < shape. When I was nearly through I very often went to the other side and with one blow finished the job, or administered a second while the tree was falling over. If the stump then displayed any ragged edges I cleaned it up with my bill-hook. After sufficient practice my wood presented clean stumps and stools instead of a series of wooden clefts and cliffs such as are found whenever a company of schoolboys have been on a job of this kind. I soon learnt not to dash at the thing with undue speed and not to hurl the whole force of my body at the tree, as it were. My technique was somewhat golfer-like. I kept my eye steadfastly on the spot I intended to strike, kept my left arm straight, did not lurch after the axe with my body and only exerted full force at the last minute when also I did some good wrist-work. (Thus I grandly write about my method, and should have done it that way, and possibly, on occasion, even did do so.) I certainly think that the secret of a good cut, especially when dealing with a medium-sized hazel bush, is in that last golfer-flick of the wrist. I was once held up for a considerable time by a ticket-collector at South Kensington Underground Station who explained to me that his particular and striking ability as a boxer was due to the fact that he didn't put out his strength till the final second of a blow. He was not a big man and he insisted the success in boxing went to the most intelligent, to men like himself who realized that force should be reserved till the last second. 'I box from here,' he kept repeating, and tapped his forehead to indicate the seat of his weightiest weapon in the ring. This unexpected pugilistic tutorial stuck in my mind, and I carried it over with some degree of success into the realm of forestry.

The great thing is to keep the axe sharp. Much depends upon the strength of mind to do this, for it saves much expense of body and spirit. I found out before it was too late (though late enough), that it is an illusion to suppose that one must take an axe to a grindstone with wheel and water complete. The ordinary hand-stone will serve if applied frequently and with a level pressure that does not merely grind the edge but the space before the edge. I used to tell myself to aim at never touching the very edge at all with the stone, but to grind down the rise behind. Given a big stone – not one broken in half – one can sharpen an axe all right and be independent of the elaborate wheel which requires two people to be on the job. For comfort with axe-work, then, I beg to prescribe a sharp edge. And secondly a good axe. That is to say an axe that is neither too heavy nor too light. This is not so simple as it sounds. There are many absurdly balanced axes about: axes with monstrously heavy blades and handles that do not balance them. I bought an axe with a fair-sized blade and a well-balanced shaft, and used it with pleasure for some time, till I was offered the use of a heavier axe. At first I thought the latter much better, and when I took up my own it seemed ridiculously light, and on using it I completely missed my aim. But I found that I couldn't possibly keep the heavy one sharp and it became temper-losingly blunt. So I went back to my old axe, and soon it gained in the weight it seemed to have lost, and I never changed again. (Have I any hint regarding a method of sharpening with the stone? Yes, take a stick, lay it on the ground, kneel down and grind away at the blades the edge of which is kept free of the ground by means of the stick.)

Here as in all these matters, to do your job properly and get pleasure from it, you need the good tool. This is equally true of the bill-hook. For a long time I was content with a light, blunt, rattling affair – thinking it all right. But one day I went out and bought a heavier one, a beauty – the gain in speed of work, cleanness of cut, and pleasure in execution being far in excess of the cash value. I generally learn this sort of thing too late, and I learnt this too late since two-thirds of my job was done before I got rid of the old bill-hook. I hadn't realized the difference it would make. The fact is we have in the bill-hook an even more delightful tool than the axe. Especially if you are thinning. You cut down a tree, after which it is necessary to clean it, that is knock off the branches and thus produce a clear pole to be taken away for firewood or any of the other purposes. This is the time when a sharp bill-hook is a joy: a single back-handed slash will generally sever the small branches, while with one or two strokes you can dispatch the larger branches; and if your pole is not too thick and you wish to cut it in half, you can still use your bill-hook for this if it is good and sharp, holding the pole in the left hand and coming down with a back-hand stroke with the right hand. This is an exercise that engages the whole body. It is difficult to think of a more delightful job than this, stripped to the waist in the sun, and thus enabled for a few too briefly passing hours to step aside from the inanities of our repellent civilization. I am writing this account while finishing off this forestry work, and since I am very near the end of the wood the thought of possibly never using a bill-hook again in a big way is very depressing. No doubt I shall be able to use an axe from time to time, and even a plough; but when shall I ever again have a whole wood to thin?

But before passing on I must mention one peculiarity about bill-hooks. They have a way of disappearing. This experience is shared by all woodmen. You are always changing over from axe to bill-hook and vice versa. You put the bill-hook down, take up the axe, and having done what you want it for, reach for the bill-hook again. It has disappeared. Often it is impossible to find it without an irritating search. True, one gets wary at last about this peculiarity and one automatically plans a conspicuous place for putting it down. But, once a more than usually strange disappearance trick was played on me. Near the end of the day's work a shower came on, and leaving my bill-hook I went a certain distance away where there was good shelter. On returning I could not find my bill-hook. In this case there were only ten square yards where it could be, an area not overgrown with anything. I searched minutely and scientifically within that given area. To no avail. It was not there. At last I went home, hoping that on the morrow it would have returned. And sure enough there it was in the morning in the middle of the space I had gone over again and again while searching for it.

4 Meditation on the Struggle for Life

During my work of clearing there was one thing which gave me particular satisfaction. This was the cutting away of the honeysuckle. Belonging to the parasitic company of plants that engage trees for climbing up instead of rising on their own accord, they often provide grim spectacles in the woods of merciless throttling and strangulation. Ascending from the bottom of the trunk they spiral their way upwards, clinging tightly to the bark. This hinders the sap, the tree's circulation, and after a year or two the young trunk itself becomes a spiral-shaded pole, bulging out in a remarkable manner as if an erect rubber tube full of air had been tightly wound with cord in spiral formation so that it bulged out between the cord (though in the case of the victimized tree or branch the bulge appears *at* the cord of honeysuckle). The tree struggles to live in spite of the stranglehold, but generally in vain. It is apt to die and rot and bend over, a parched ruin upon which the honeysuckle thrives, spurning the base degrees by which it did ascend. I have come upon portions of the wood where honeysuckle had practically taken over: the captive, the twisted, the mutilated, the dying, the dead ash trees stood hopelessly entangled in the network of ropes, pulleys, nooses, loops, ligatures, lassos which outwardly appeared as lifeless themselves as pieces of cord, but were centrally bursting with life and power, ready and willing to pull down the wood.

Mr Aldous Huxley once suggested that if Wordsworth had lived in the tropics he would not have written about Nature in the way he did. This is pretty obvious. Such speculations are not very fruitful; we cannot move in these hypothetical fields with any profundity. In the tropics Wordsworth would not have written his known work, and perhaps none at all; but that does not mean that men who are native to that clime may not find an approach to a total vision of the Absolute. It also begs the question that if Wordsworth had not been capable of total truth, Nature, in England, as elsewhere, provides ample opportunity for the half-truth. The king of the half-vision is that other lordly and everlasting bard, Thomas Hardy. In one of his forest descriptions in *The*

Woodlanders, after speaking of Nature's merciless battles, he adds – 'Here, as everywhere, the Unfulfilled Intention, which makes life what it is, was as obvious as it could be among the depraved crowds of a city slum. The leaf was deformed, the curve was crippled, the taper was interrupted; the lichen ate the vigour of the stalk, and the ivy slowly strangled to death the promising sapling.' I came across the same sort of thing every day in my wood. It could make me silent and it could make me sad, but personally I cannot see the spectacle in terms of unfulfilled intention save superficially. What I see is – an almost liquid surging up of life. I see that life as a massive unity, moving and flowering under the influence of Fire – the air itself taking visible shape in the plants. Some of it does not get up, all of it cannot get up. But if one tree succeeds, one baby survives, I applaud.

Thus, even when we are feeling gloomy, philosophy will keep breaking in, with its happy, glancing gleam.

The spectacle in my wood which fascinated me most, and encouraged me most, was – decomposition. As I hacked my way through the undergrowth I came upon many fallen trees which had been lying on the ground for years. They lay there presenting every variety of rotting trunk and bough, in every stage of transition as they slowly burnt their way back into the ashes from which the Phoenix of Life rises up again. I would take my bill-hook and cut into a trunk lying covered with moss. It would go in deep as easily as into a lump of cake, until it struck abruptly the inner part not yet decayed. I would take out slices, letting them crumble in my hand and fall to the ground – as *humus*. Once a seed, then a sapling, then a great hard tree, now softly turning into *earth*. I found them, I say, in every shape and style, lying in the silent shades in a melancholy mightier than beauty. At a touch a branch would fall, already dust. Under my feet a weeping clod of wood damply squelched like wet paper. Deep, soft, dark green moss covered nearly every limb, like velvet on old discarded furniture. Age or storm had laid these low, but there were also stumps where full-grown trees had once been sawn off. I was never tired of testing their present status with my boots. Some were still hard as a table, with perhaps a large fungus growing on them, nearly the size, colour, and shape of an elephant's ear. Others, enmossed inches deep, were as springy to stand or sit on as an armchair. Some had almost wholly conformed to the law of return and scarcely differed in appearance or material from the earth around. Others made magnificent portals and main entrances to rabbits' burrows.

Sometimes I knelt down beside one of the most ancient trunks, and peered under the bark and into the caves and recesses and cups that marked the erosion of time; and there I found colonies of insects building their Jerusalem in these countries of decay which must represent for them the acme of perfection. And there also fungi, like jellyfish, like sponges, like rubber flowers, took life-giving elixir from the burning bark. And as I sat and leaned and looked upon these lands it seemed to me that here too was blessedness and peace, and glory though it did not shine, and innocence untainted as the new-born babe. Here might the weary and the sick come and lay them down; and without anguish, and without misgiving, fall back and return to the ashes that never die.

5 *The Virtues of Hazel*

As I advanced, the terms 'hard-wood' and 'soft-wood' began to mean something definite to me now, for the difference in resistance to the axe was decisive. There were a few spruce trees at the edge and my axe sank into that wood very easily. The extreme softness of young oak surprised me. The hazel was by no means as hard as the ash. All the same I was puzzled by these terms; for we all know how hard the oak is when seasoned, and the spruce becomes excellent, I understand, for rafters and boarding, ladders, props, and packing-cases. That miserable tree, the elder, which occasionally I came across, can be cut without effort, but seems to become harder even than any of the others. The axe makes a different sound against each species of tree, and a skilled woodman ought to be able to tell from a distance whether, say, an ash or a hazel is being cut down.

It is easier to get your axe into a hazel than an ash; but it is much harder to get at the hazel. It gave me little pleasure to come upon a row of hazel bushes to be cut down and laid. The hazel does not aspire. A dozen shoots from an ash-stool will seek the perpendicular, and the most favourably placed amongst them will stand up straight and high. But the shoots, fifty or more some-times, from the hazel-stool, while they *start* straight, later begin to fan out, and even the one at the centre makes no attempt to grow straight, and all the branches intertwine tremendously. In short the hazel is a bush, not a tree; and a bush is a tree whose shoots thrive in concert and together make the unit. The hazels' quick growth, abundance, flexibility, and thinness make them one of the most valuable of all timber crops, since they can be twisted so easily into fences and hurdles, while their tributary twigs are the very thing for bean-stakes.

I imagine that they are also excellent for fishing-rods. I do not know whether this is officially right but I think it must be, because certain branches that I handled *were* fishing-rods. While at work I caught fish with them in my own peculiar way. When you cut down hazel you do not clean it for firewood or poles (unless the bush is hugely overgrown with shoots the size of small trees). You lay the branches on the ground all facing one way, placing each branch behind and half over the previous one, so that when you are dealing with many bushes you make a long line of sloping hazel branches like a kind of hedge which is called a drift. It is pleasant to transform the tangle into drifts running parallel through the cleaned-up wood. But to lay them thus is not very easy. The numerous tributary twigs of hazel bushes are so intertwined that when you start to extract the branch you have just cut off, it is no easy matter getting it free from the main clump; and if you have left anything within reach on the ground, say a coat or a hat or a handkerchief, then often the terminal twigs of the extracted branch, bending down, will tend to scoop up your property. Once when struggling to lay a long flexible rod beside the other branches on the ground, I hooked up my hat exactly as if it were a special kind of fish. I mention this trivia because it is my only fishing story, and it would seem to suggest that here is the perfect material for the complete fisherman's rod.

It serves another purpose which also may not be official. It is splendid for the amateur chimney-sweep. Nowadays if one wants anything done one must do it oneself. To be my own plumber is quite beyond me, and when my only tap – a short one from the rain-tub to the copper – split in a frost, I never had even that one tap to use. But having once set my chimney on fire I saw that in future I must keep it swept. So taking a tip from a countryman who is full of ways and wiles, I did my own sweeping. The tip was to select a long hazel-rod of fair strength and much flexibility and take it home. Then tie a number of sprigs of holly round the thin end. This was the sweeping-brush. It was too long to fit into the room, so one just let it in from the door or window and then curved it up the chimney. Such a rod easily reached to the top of my chimney. As I cleaned lower and lower I cut the rod, thus greatly facilitating the thoroughness of the brushing. By this means the soot came down perfectly. Half-an-hour's job. And having taken the precaution of wearing gloves, an old hat, and mackintosh, I did not emerge from it in the least grimed. I do not say that this would work in a big house, but it is the chimney-sweeping solution for anyone with a cottage in the country; and so I think we must definitely give such brushes a prominent place on the list of the hazel tree's gifts to mankind.

6 In the Primeval Chase

The atmosphere of the wood was entirely altered by my intervention. It became a different place: not the same place altered, but as different as if on going down a lane to see a certain wood in a given country, you came upon another landscape. There was now no disorder, the trees were visible, and (before I had done) you could look for a long way in all directions through a small forest, whereas before you could only see a few yards. Space and light and orderliness had been introduced. It now seemed more alive, happy, and beautiful – from the view-point of man (who sticks on the labels). And since we do stick on labels it is a sad ineptitude to suppose that Nature cannot be improved upon from a 'beauty' point of view, by man. The idea that 'every prospect pleases, while only man is vile' is not the whole truth. Man has added to the beauty of Nature in as measurable a degree as, say, between an area of uneven, tufted, coarse grass and a well-tended lawn margined by geraniums.

I often used to think of this when I strayed beyond my wood into further forest-land, especially one portion which seemed to have been neglected for centuries. It was a gloomy place at most times of the year. The trees were chiefly oak with some silver birch. It was like walking at the bottom of the ocean and continually finding some wrecked vessel. Or again, like coming upon the scene of a battle waged long ago: huge corpses of tree-trunks sprawled on the ground, their limbs like the broken arms of giant men lying where they fell. From some ancient oaks, a great branch, through weight of years, violence of storm, or stroke of lightning, had cracked at the fork and the branch leaned to the ground – a giant arm with fingers gripping the earth. Often it seemed as if I had visited the place of some terrible calamity long since closed in the withered page of history, and now made ghostly by the ever-reigning silence which I dared not break. I could see little of the greenery above, but walked submerged down there amongst the dereliction and dismay of lost causes and abandoned hope. How different all this would look, I pondered, if it were taken in hand by man.

The silver birch were not doing well amongst the oak trees. Many of them were dead – blasted poles erect in the foliage of other trees. Some, still in feeble leaf, had begun to fall over, and remained on the slant, upheld by surrounding branches, looking as if they had fainted but were just caught in time. A number of trunks lay about on the ground, short pieces nearly covered over by the dog's mercury. One of these had a hole in it which ramified in several directions, at the entrance of which was a damp, round fungus; or so I thought, till I noticed it was breathing, and saw it was a large slug. This old trunk lay at the foot of an erect log – I cannot call it a tree for the trunk had broken off about ten feet from the ground. There it stood now, immensely lichened and mossed, a shaky column with one exceptional fea-ture – it had steps placed in spiral-shaped form going up. They were small steps but very attractive in their wonderful colour congruity with the weather-washed, old, white-patched bark of the birch. Had they been firm enough they would have served me admirably for climbing up to examine the top of the column. But they could hardly hold me since they were made of fungus. Nevertheless I have never seen more definite and attractive steps than those upon that tottering tower.

It is not surprising that there was an ancient atmosphere about this place, for I was working in the middle of Cranbourne Chase. At one time it had a perimeter of over eighty miles, from Shaftesbury to Salisbury on the north, and encircled by the Stour and the Avon at the other sides. Now it is shrunk to a small oasis of wild country. But that oasis has changed little in the course of centuries. It remains, as Thomas Hardy has written, 'a truly venerable track of forest land, one of the few remaining woodlands in England of undoubted primeval date, wherein Druidical mistletoe is still found on aged oaks, and where enormous yew trees, not planted by the hand of man, grow as they had grown when they were pollarded for bows'. Wandering here I could well feel that if the world is too much with my fellows it was not too much with me. In the strange days in which we live I could actually say farewell to the world far more effectually among these shades and natural debris than on any island in the Pacific Ocean.

I decided that if ever I were a fugitive from the Law this is where I would hide. But I learn that this decision of mine is not strikingly original. In fact, before 1830, the Chase had become so popular as a smuggler resort, and so sought after by thieves, murderers, and criminals of every grade no less than by poachers, blackmailers, tramps, and vagabonds, that in the end it was treated as a covert for crime, and was disafforested.

7 Bracken

You have to keep your eyes open in the country if you want to see the spring before it is all over. This is borne in on me every year. The whole affair is so swift and so variegated that unless we are careful we miss half of it. During some months of summer and some of winter the casual eye sees little change, but during April and May the speed of appearance and disappearance is almost on a par with the cinema. One wants to see the show through again at once, and get the order of things right. Nothing requires more deliberate intellectual exertion that to follow the unfolding closely, nothing more time-eating. I found it much easier just to get on with my job of thinning, and I often put off looking at something until 'later' – by which time it was gone. Luckily the flowers do not all appear quite at once. The primrose path has time to make an impression before it becomes the property of bugle and ground-ivy; the celandines, the anemones, and the violets have fallen before the bluebells rise to spread their gospel and then yield to the aristocracy of the foxglove.

In this wood it always seemed to me at one period, near the end of May, that everything would have to give way to the empire of dog's mercury. But of course this was reckoning without the bracken which steps in and takes control from June onwards. Here indeed is a case in which you must keep awake if you are not to be surprised at almost an apparition. For the unfurling of these fern-flags from their unnoticed beginnings to great thickness and height is one of the swiftest of all the transactions. The leaves are packed in a roll very much like those things you find in Christmas crackers and blow out. And they unroll so swiftly that their internal chemical apparatus might seem to have the force of steam. Unlike ordinary ferns and all the other plants around, they continue to grow higher and higher until six or eight feet is not uncommon. A miniature forest has suddenly appeared in which a child might get lost.

Farmers can very seldom enjoy aesthetically what they deplore agriculturally, and since bracken has a very bad reputation as a particularly injurious weed, we seldom hear anything good of it. But a philosophic mind, uninstructed in the claims of agriculture, might well conceive the frond in a favourable light. For it is a direct descendant of those Tree-Ferns that once covered the whole land of Europe before bird, quadruped, or man appeared. The atmosphere was then unbreathable, containing in suspension in the state of poisonous gas, the huge mass of carbon which has since become coal. The tree-ferns cleansed it. They subtracted the carbon, storing it in their leaves and stems. They continued this atmospheric purification for generations, and when at last they died their buried remnants became coal in which even today we can find many leaves and stems wonderfully preserved, archives in which we may read 'the history of this ancient vegetation which has given us an atmosphere that we can breathe and has stored up for us in the bowels of the earth those strata of coal which are the wealth of nations'. Fabre, from whom I quote those words, traces bracken as descending from that noble line, and states that 'the stem of our common Bracken reproduces in its bundles of blackish, lignous tissue, the rather sketchy design of a two-headed, heraldic eagle as though to blazen the nobility of its ancient race.'

And should the man of philosophic mind, while contemplating these things, fall into a less elevated mood and inquire whether it was really worthwhile for the ferns to cleanse the air of carbon poison gas if we, the inheritors of their bounty, prepare a poison gas of our own to destroy ourselves, he may still reflect that Necessity, so aptly called the mother of invention and discovery, has in these latter days found uses for bracken unsuspected by our ancestors. Thus the Glasgow Research Station finds that silage can be made from it. Mr Ronald Duncan cooks it as a kind of asparagus. Dr Krebs of Sheffield University claims that yeast can be made out of it. The Germans make petrol from it. Silage for stock, petrol for machines, yeast and salad for men – not bad for a weed.

Not bad; and a hopeful sign of the times with regard to the future. A new principle is beginning to be advanced – that of each country making use of its own resources before dashing off to the ends of the earth for new materials. Hitherto we have tapped our own resources only to a small extent, and when we saw something in a far country we built a ship and went and got it from there. Other nations have followed suit, all trying at once to procure the rare substance from the far place, and claiming 'equal right' to do so. That was called Imperialism. Today a new possibility opens. Science steps forward demonstrating in a remarkably concrete way that since all things are all things, almost anything can be made from anything. Before our astonished gaze they turn wood into jumpers, milk into buttons, maize into mud-guards, glass into shirts, bracken into petrol. The dream of the old alchemists is surpassed and transmutation becomes the order of the day. No longer shall Imperialism be necessary. No longer shall men, in the name of trade, in the name of religion, in the name of civilization go to Persia, to India, to Honolulu in order to steal away some local treasure. They shall stoop down and find it at their feet.

In the meanwhile I am more content to regard bracken as bracken, and not as petrol or anything else. Indeed I fear that if I am right about future developments, men will look at phenomena even less than they do today. To *look at* the object, at any object, and see it in its own right is the key to a fuller apprehension of the mystery and significance of life. But there is no money in this, and so people do not bother to use their eyes in that way. Perhaps in the future they may look at the object more closely – but only with the motive of turning it into something else.

Let me look at my bracken here, I said to myself, without ulterior motive or agricultural disgust, and watch it spring up mushroom-like before my very eyes. Most of the flowers have already faded and now they are disappearing beneath the ferns, and the great kingdom of dog's mercury no longer usurps the scene. And as I gaze at it I gaze back across the years of my life and see again the tall bracken in the lonely glen on the Wicklow Mountains through which deer and stags leap with amazing speed.

8 *Old and New Attitude to Trees*

This wood had been neglected so long that I came upon great waste of potential timber. Here and there a full-grown tree had evidently crashed down upon surrounding shoots. I occasionally found a trunk or a big branch lying right across a stool from which ten shoots were growing. All would be twisted, none worth keeping there. Many of these young ash trees had thereby assumed the strangest shapes, for they had had to twist themselves as if they were made of rubber. Sometimes they looked like the neck plus the head of a swan, and I saw one that reminded me of that queer flamingo that Alice used as a croquet-mallet in Wonderland. Some had twisted their way up snake-wise in order to pass the obstructions. Some were linked in close embrace and one had grown in such an extraordinary way that it now *ran through* a larger stem. I could do nothing in such places but get rid of all the twisters and leave an open space.

At other times I came upon three or four excellent trees, all straight, all doing well, all big and high. But since they were too near to one another, only one could be left standing, and I had to select the best. I was often in a real quandary in deciding which was the best, for just as at one place I would find three to five twisters closer together, at another I would find an equal number of champions.

When it was thus necessary to axe a beautiful ash tree for no better reason than that it was too close to another one, I felt extremely apologetic. For trees do exert a strong personality. It is said that in certain parts of Austria there are still to be found peasants who beg the pardon of a tree before felling it. Sir James Frazer told how the inhabitants of Sumatra used to lay the blame at the door of the Dutch authorities. A native would go to a tree which he had to cut down in order to make a road, and would pretend to pick up a letter which he then read aloud to the effect that the Dutch authorities enjoined him to fell the trees . . . 'You hear that, Spirits,' he would cry, 'I must begin clearing at once, or I shall be hanged.' The seriousness of tree-worship in ancient Germany brought ferocious penalties upon anyone who peeled the bark of a standing tree: his navel was cut and nailed to the tree, and he was driven round and round it until his guts were twisted about the trunk. Plutarch relates how the withering of a sacred fig-tree in Athens or Rome was regarded with consternation; while if a tree was observed by someone to be drooping, a hue and cry was set up and people rushed to its assistance with buckets of water as if to put out a fire. At many times and places it was considered essential to make sacrifices to trees sometimes with fowls, and sometimes with human beings. If we bear in mind the many beneficent qualities ascribed to trees in the past, it is easy to understand why a custom like the May tree or the May-pole prevailed. In spring a tree was brought into the village amidst applause and rejoicing, the intention being to bring home to the village and to each house the blessings which the tree-spirit had the power to bestow.

Mankind dominates the world today. It is certain that trees once did so. It is not possible for us even to imagine the immense forests that existed at the dawn of history – when clearings were but tiny islands in the atlantic stretches of wood. In the first century the Hercynian Forest stretched eastward from the Rhine farther than any man knew: men, questioned by Caesar, had travelled for two months without reaching the end. I like to think how the Weald of Kent, Surrey, and Sussex are remnants of the great forest of Anderida that once clothed the whole of the south-eastern portion of the island, joining another (older than the Chase or father of it) from Hampshire to Devon – and how in the reign of Henry II the citizens of London hunted the wild boar and bull in the woods of Hampstead.

However, since the days of tree-domination and tree-worship we have progressed so much that we now can see them in terms of £.s.d. When I cut down a tree I had levelled a piece of 'timber' valued at so much a foot. During many a five minutes I have knocked out about a shilling's worth a minute. I stacked the poles neatly in piles of a hundred – (my own pay being so much a 'lug'). One day a timber-merchant came to the woods to decide what he wanted to buy. He was accompanied by the foreman of the estate. Together they arrived at the just price. Then the timber-merchant inspected a portion of the wood not yet tackled by me, marking specially straight trees that he fancied. I said in an aside to the foreman that not all the ones the man was marking could rightly come down, and the foreman said to the merchant at intervals – 'But we must look after our own interests.' The man took no notice and continued marking trees while we looked on disapprovingly, the foreman repeating – 'Of course we must look after our own interests.'

When the timber-merchant had gone, the foreman, an unexuberant personality, looked round at the wood, appraising it. 'There baint nothing in trees,' he said. I made some kind of commercial remark. He looked round at the wood again and finally dismissed the whole prospect with two weighty words – 'It's *dead money*,' he said. Having brought forth this gem of ages-old wisdom he gazed over the wood sourly and mournfully as if filled with sorrow at the sight of so much dead money.

9 Clothes and Sanity

It was not until the bracken had started to appear that the roof was put on the wood. Since the ash does not send out its branches till near the top, we do get this effect of a roof in any reasonable ash wood. Visualize a larch, a chestnut tree, and many a beech and oak, and then remember the tall, bare trunks of the ash branching only at their crowns, and you will grant that it is indeed the placing on of a high roofing that we witness in May and June. It was pleasant to look through an acreage of bare trunks that I had disentangled from the press of competition, and then up at the intermingling greenery enlightened by the sun. You can seldom get this effect from other trees growing together. The chestnut branches out very low, and while beeches do often present a high, lone stem they often do not, and you see beautiful leafy branches sweeping the ground; while the oak, though also capable of the long clean trunk, goes in for great thick limbs sprawling out parallel with the ground or twisting upwards from a low fork. However, I must not run my image of columns upholding a roof too far in connection with my ash, for there were many gaps of course between the crowns, and also a number of blanks owing to lack of trees.

I welcomed these gaps and blanks, for otherwise I had to work in the shade far too often. And when the sun is shining I do not take kindly to working in the shade. Give me heat every time, I do not mind how much. I can do twice the amount of work in the sun than when away from it, or clothed off from it. This is partly due to my attitude towards clothes. I like to wear the right thing in the right place, and am no advocate of unconventional attire. But the right thing, at certain times, in certain places for many people, is often a pair of shorts and nothing more except for the feet. For many agricultural jobs that is not the right thing at all, but for some it is. As for axe-work in the summer, and bill-hook work while cleaning your fallen tree, it certainly is right when the weather is hot or muggy or showery. Thus unencumbered I can do, and like doing, a week's work in two days. The hotter I get the harder I work, perspiration making me almost cold and the sun not hot enough to make me even feel its heat then. The sheer freedom of the limbs with the breeze on the body gives a pleasure not easily excelled; one could justifiably enthuse about it; I content myself with saying that though this is not the only way of feeling happy and alive, it is one way. To use the mind at full concentration is one of the most manly things we can do, since this capacity happens to be the special gift of man; but we are also animals, and we experience great joy when, in primitive surroundings, we are not dolled up and tied down with artificial skins. Thus with me anyway; I cannot exaggerate the satisfaction I get from becoming a 'savage' – even in colour. And I fear that many a Lancashire young man – need I say 'lad'? – having come home from the Far East, will miss, at intervals throughout his life, sometimes quite savagely, his shirtless army days in the jungle.

There exists a strange crowd of people called Nudists. It might be thought that here we have sane people in an over-civilized world. But this is not so. They are misled. They imagine that by simply taking off their clothes they can side-step the sophistications of metropolitanism. Yet of course they can do nothing of the sort, they merely become unclothed and in their wrong minds. Once I turned off a main street in London, and having paid a fee of two shillings, was admitted into a large house in which a nudist gathering was in progress. When standing in the porch and glancing round at the pavemented vistas of the metropolis, I felt surprise at the assumption that inside this house it would be possible to 'return to nature' by the mere removal of clothes. And having entered I did not find the scene or the proceedings in any degree inspiring. There was one room reserved for games, though no particular games were being played and people were wandering about in it aimlessly since there was no possibility of exercise of an exacting sort. Most of the members were in the next room – having tea and cakes. No one wore anything. This looked incongruous in the electric-lit room with its tea and cakes and the people sitting in rows – idiotic might be a better word. And should anyone have come along, I reflected, with an erotic *arrière pensée*, he or she would quickly have found that nudism is the enemy of eroticism (though possibly not if everyone wore a mask). As I had entered fairly unnoticed it was easy to slip away without offence, and I was glad indeed to regain the comparative sanity of the city streets.

The point is that these nudists run a principle – no clothes: (and this insistence upon none at all is an indignity). It is just a thoughtless principle with no sense in it, seen in practice to be far the most unnatural and unsane affair in the whole city – a sort of climax of absurdity. The more reasonable, open-air nudists do at least enjoy the sun. Unfortunately they sun-bathe. That is to say they *lie about* doing nothing. In moderation that is all right, of course, but done in company and as a great thing in itself, it is pretty miserable. The whole thing is done too seriously and too thoroughly. One should avoid thoroughness in such fields. My own principle concerning the whole matter is simply this – that the way to enjoy the sun is through working in it or playing a game in it, and that there should never be the raising of an eyelid if a shirt is removed in any congruous setting.

But today we still have crazy people who think nothing of a bather approaching the sea in bathing-shorts, but would stare at a cyclist going up a steep hill on a hot day in shorts only. And then over against this we have the lunacy of a whole-hogging nakedness carried even into a city mansion during a winter evening!

In my wood it was unnecessary to consider the existence of either sort of person. I could do the natural thing without the slightest botheration. Much of the work was really strenuous. There were trees to cut down large enough to merit two men with a saw; and when I had axed them down, and cleaned them up, and then chopped them into poles short enough to load on a lorry, I arranged them in piles of a hundred. All this was wonderful exercise, the axing and the hauling about requiring full strength, while the branch-clearing with the bill-hook as I held up the heavier branch with one hand, engaged every muscle in the body. It gave me unbounded pleasure to go at this furiously for hours on end if the sun was blazing down on me. It didn't matter how hot it was, the hotter the better, for then I became very wet with perspiration and needed the warmth of the sun as one coming out of water, while if it rained the drops melted at once. Thus dressed I often felt that I could go on all day without exhaustion, whereas in the winter I couldn't do a third of the work in the time. I used to smile sometimes at the thought that I was being paid to enjoy myself thus, in a world where a boss who says – 'I'm not paying you to enjoy yourself, my boy!' is considered a particularly reasonable and high-minded pillar of society.

10 *The Garden of Eden*

That was one peak of pleasure. But I got as much out of sitting down for my breaks. To be tired enough to make the act of sitting down a sensation of real relief is a pleasure which has much to be said for it. And provided that you are not over-exhausted but just physically in need of a rest – then the mind often functions at its very best. After some food, hot tea from the thermos, and a cigarette, it is quite remarkable how freely the brain can move, and how favourable the conditions are for unpremeditated meditation.

There is one more proviso for me – the perfect seat in a sunny spot: or in a shady spot at those hours on certain summer days when the sun is actually too hot to sit in. I was expert at finding such places. I kept finding new ones, thinking each better than the last. By a perfect place I mean a tree which I could lean against comfortably and which was so situated that other trees would not block the sun at those times when I would be sitting down. As I say, I found several, and shall remember them all my life because of the happiness I found there and the glory that shone round me. There was one outstanding tree at the foot of which I took up my position very often. I did not cut my way towards it for some time, but when I had discovered it I made it my headquarters for meditation. Trees are particularly conducive to meditation: no doubt that famous Bo-tree did much to prepare Gautama for his hour of enlightenment.

This particular tree was not an ash, it was a fine old oak. Its trunk had considerable girth – three men holding hands could hardly surround it. At about three feet up it leant out and forked into such large branches that it was a question which might claim to be the trunk. At this fork, and for some distance along one of the branches, a fern garden was flourishing. (This arboreal garden was very delightful to contemplate in the summer. A maple tree, not far off, had a mistletoe growing on one of its branches, and on my way to Blandford I used to stop and look at another maple where to my amazement I saw a young silver birch growing healthily in a moist niche high up.) The arrangement of branches was such that no great limb immediately roofed me blocking out the sun, but at a suitable height the leafage was so plentiful that as a shelter from rain this was perhaps the best tree I have ever known. That leafage, combined with the trunk which gently sloped outwards over me, prevented a drop of water from falling on me for quite a long time even when it was raining heavily outside. I say outside because on such occasions I could sit as if I were indoors without the slightest necessity to put on a coat. It was curious to see the rain pouring down while I, though out-of-doors, was really in-doors. It would be half an hour before the roof would begin to leak a bit.

The situation was not altogether perfect with regard to the sunshine, for after ten o'clock in the morning a big tree intervened. But up till then it was the best place in the wood, and during really hot weather it was superb for thoughtful shade. If there was wind at other places there was no wind here, for I placed 'drifts' either of hazel or of branches cut from my ash-poles, at each side. And finally, it was easy to lean against: the earth was soft and no roots stuck out; instead there was a sort of alcove into which I could fit and lean back so as to be comfortably upright.

I mention all these particulars because the reader will then recognize that since I also got a long view, a long sloping-down view of the wood and further woods beyond, seeing nothing but trees, and having behind me and at each side nothing but trees, I was in a highly favourable position, indeed a position in which not only happy hours but inspired and fruitful hours might be spent.

During the late spring and summer the sun fell upon this spot between 8 a.m. and 10 a.m. And as this was between six and eight normal time, the temperature of the sunlight could not have been improved upon. Since my job was being done on the basis of piece-work I was in command of my own time. On beautiful mornings my ideal was to do early work on the wood and sit down here for breakfast at eight when the sun had reached the oak. I took up my position carefully, back upright, head against trunk, legs straight out, with half-empty haver-sack under the knees, and a dry coat or sack to sit on, arms folded or hands clasped between knees. *Then* I immediately forgot my body, abandoned it – and became all spirit or soul or mind or whatever it is that sits inside us looking out of our two windows.

And now, at this point – to justify the foregoing details – I would gladly tell you what then I knew, what then I grasped. Ah, could I but do so, then would I have the power to bless and to save, even as I was saved and blessed! But I did not quite grasp it, I did not understand the Knowledge that seemed mine. As I strove, and strove again to penetrate the meaning of the glory and the promise in the scene around, and to frame into a conception something that I seemed to *know* – it eluded me, it always just drew back. Sometimes it came very close, as if it were about three feet above my head, at times almost brushing my forehead – but not coming in, and soon fading far away again. This experience of the Undeclared Announcement trembling on the verge of utterance, was imaged by Thoreau in terms of an eagle – 'an eagle that suddenly comes into the field of view, suggesting great things and thrilling the beholder, as if it were bound hitherward with a message for me; but it comes no nearer, but circles and soars away growing dimmer, disappointing me, till it is lost behind a cliff or a cloud'.

Yet something was clear to me, and I will set down here one note which I took as the nearest I could get to my finding – I turn off the road, enter the wood, and sit down under the tree. The sun gleams upon everything, there is glittering and shining everywhere. A green caterpillar is lowered down by an invisible thread in front of me, and as it swings about, the sun shines through its transparency. A little distance off a spider mounts upwards on another unseen rope, as if slowly falling upwards by inverse gravitation or being drawn up by an invisible crane, while another calmly walks on the air, and yet another takes a seat upon nothing. A bush over there is glittering with rain-drops, little white lanterns fastened to the lower side of twigs; but if I swing my head slightly to one side, some of those lights turn colour, becoming red and purple. A creature alights on the back of my hand: its body being in the shape of a tiny solid canoe, which has one high brown sail rather out of proportion to the boat; suddenly the sail opens into two sails using the body at the base as a hinge, and the whole thing flies away – a butterfly, like a flying flower. Then there is the ground I sit on, the tree behind me, and the trees around me, and the flowers, and the thing I can't see, the air, yet stronger as a substance than, say, an aeroplane or a liner. A general voice is given to the whole thing by the birds. Most of this is incomprehensible to me, and even if a learned man describes what is going on and how it is all done, he will not be explaining it for me. And the interesting thing about it is that it *works*. Here we have nothing but a series of the most curious kind of miraculous activities and queer appearances and extravagant shapes, but it all works in concert. One might suppose that it could possibly work for a month or so or even a year – but it does it every year, it goes on working without mishap and without running down. This in itself fills me with a great deal of confidence and some comfort. Added to this there is the general look of the place and the spirit in the atmosphere. Indeed we have all been so struck with its aspect that we have invented a word for it – beauty. I am surrounded here with law, order, and beauty, and am myself absolutely happy here. There is nothing to make me unhappy. No evil thing meets my eye, there is nothing bad here. I begin to grasp the obvious fact that this place is – perfect. And suddenly I realize where I am! I am in the Garden of Eden. I had heard about it always as a definite place in the past. There was no error in speaking of the Garden as existing, but the mistake lay in tying it down in time and place. For it still exists – all we need is the key of the gate. The first two persons in history dwelt in the Garden, it is said. But they ate of the Tree of Knowledge and had to go. That must be the truth: at the birth of consciousness we became *onlookers* and were separated from Nature, and left the Garden to create a world of our own apart from Nature. Our next step is a further extension of consciousness when we shall realize the unity of life on a higher plane of understanding. Having tasted of *that* tree of knowledge we shall enter the Garden of Eden once more, and Paradise shall be regained.

11 Ode to the Sun and to Idleness

It is true that at times I sought to pierce the mystery and to grasp the truth that seemed within my reach. But very often I refrained from thinking as much as possible, wishing just to receive what was given and glory in it. I certainly set myself against irrelevant thoughts, and against evil thoughts and thoughts of bitterness or annoyance concerning the outside world, which often pursued me into the wood like loathsome hounds. To think such things here would be fearful waste of time, I felt – the precious moments must not be lost. Here there was no need to think evil or to do evil, just as there was no chance of seeing evil. It was enough merely to sit in the sun.

To sit in the sun. This is still one of the greatest experiences of life for us in the West. And it is free. No millionaire can buy up the sun and sell it to us. All the inventions through all the centuries have added nothing to this gladness, nor may any frantic folly take it away. The poor deluded multitude, dungeoned and depraved by lunatics and magnates, may prefer *artificial* sunshine, but the real thing is there all the same, and cannot be taken down.

Pardon me if on this theme I speak with some slight intemperance. I am not quite normal in my love of the sun. It has always been a passion with me, I cannot call it less. To this day I remember the feeling of outrage I experienced when, in the schoolroom, on the sun shining in, the schoolmaster would get up and *draw down the blind*. I remember thinking the man must be crazy. 'Already I began to love the sun; a boy I loved the sun, Not as I since have loved him, as a pledge And surety of our earthly life,' said Wordsworth, 'But for this cause, that I had seen him lay His beauty on the morning hills.' Thus also have I loved the sun: because of his pledge, and because of his light upon the hill; but also because he transforms me – within no less than without.

Especially in March. Then the air is still chilly, but the sun is warm again – February's feeble ray is suddenly doubled, and sometimes if we can shelter from the cold wind we can get really warm. We are cold, and when the black cloud passes across, we shiver. Then the sun emerges from the silvered margin, the glowing ball comes out and blazes down upon us. At this moment I *give myself* to the experience. I close my eyes, and it is as if a warm velvet glove were laid across my face, an invisible blanket wrapped around me. We call it heat. But what is that? Am I taken in the arms of God? Everything is transformed, this is holy ground, even I am holy, my heart is purged of sin, I forgive everything, I love all things, I am lifted up; and in understanding I pass beyond all theory, all system, resting utterly content in this blessing and this sign – worshipping the sun as if it were God himself, or at least his regent chaired beside the throne.

I have said I sat in the sun, but more often I *lay* in it – sideways, head on haversack (I cannot lie on my back). As a matter of fact I often take up this position – lying sideways – when I'm intellectually stuck over something and want to concentrate. But here I often did it because I wanted to sleep. The thing was to get as tired as possible, either by going to bed late or through strenuous work, and then lie in the sun – again especially in March or April – and go to sleep. I chose some particular spot at the foot of an ash to which the sun came and at each side of which I had placed drifts. At the chosen moment I lay down, curled up, and closed my eyes while the sun shone on my face. Often a strong, chilly wind blew, but it didn't come near me, I received only the sun. Then I entered my own special, simple paradise. I was absolutely tucked away from the world – several miles in all directions from it – I was totally hidden from sight of mortal soul, and no one knew where I was nor would be coming anywhere near me. I was free from the entire turmoil of the world. I lay there, almost sinking into, melting into the earth, waiting for sleep to come and take me right down – wondering if death in reality is more than such a joyous sinking down as this. But truly now I indulged in no thoughts, no metaphysical speculations, I became little higher than an animal – and no lower. I laughed to think what a reprehensible sight I would have made to any *busy* man who came upon me there, a sloping slacker, an untoiling son of earth! But I felt no need to offer up apologies to the unreproving Beings around. Let the world outside carry on, I would say, let them dash hither and thither, let them kill one another wholesale, let them go to hell, I'm wrapped in the embrace of Nature and filled with peace and love! And like any dog, like any savage, I lay there enjoying myself, harming no man, selling nothing, competing not at all, thinking no evil, smiled on by the sun, bent over by the trees, and softly folded in the arms of the earth.

12 Birds and Animals in the Wood

On such occasions I became so much part of the general furniture of the wood that my presence was not noticed by bird or animal. One day I was disturbed by a loud hammering on the oak tree. It came from a very small bird with a large beak. Then it flew to an ash, took up a position on a dead-looking branch and began hammering again – real hard strokes of the beak, not pecking but hitting. Then up to another place, a junction of branches and out of sight, from where I heard more hammering, and then in sight again higher up – exactly as if the bird was on business as a carpenter come to test the tree and knock in a few nails where necessary. It sometimes flew up, but more often walked up. After having made a thorough examination it descended the trunk, walking down backwards the whole way, quite oblivious of Newton's law, and knocking as it went along just as if it considered the decorative lichen needed some nailing down.

I wondered why it pecked so hard, since it would surely be difficult to catch hold of an insect that way. But bird authorities say that the insect in question is well behind the rotten bark and the beak has to pierce its way there. But how then does it see the insect to be picked up? The bird was obviously a woodpecker, I thought. But no, it was a nuthatch, a near relation. For the method of descending the tree, *walking* down either backwards or head first, distinguishes it: this mode of descent is evidently reserved for the nuthatch alone. Moreover, the woodpecker is inclined to make less of a hammering noise than a rattling; once when I heard one doing its stuff it sounded like a tractor-driver changing gear badly.

I know very little about birds, and I do not attempt to sort them out at all extensively, being content to watch them fly. The centuries pass, but we are just as fascinated as ever by these creatures who don't know what it is to *fall*, but go from the top of one tree to another upon the roads of air. They must be happy up there, we feel, housed in nests on trees, and able to pass along not in an aeroplane but as an aeroplane. But no one should even superficially compare a bird with an aeroplane: to figure such a thing one would have to imagine a bird whose outspread wings have got permanently stuck, and whose beak is a propeller. Yet the aeroplane shares this with birds – that it is a lover of woods. It is strange how pilots cannot resist the temptation to swoop down low over the tree-tops. On one particular occasion, a truly enormous and dark aeroplane passed just touching the tops of the trees above me: first the sudden thundering roar, then the flashing past of the huge structure. It was so colossal, so extreme a case, that I was driven right back across the centuries and saw myself as an Early Man in the jungle startled by the miraculous appearance of a flying monster, and dashing off to join the amazed and affrighted tribe.

I have nothing new to impart about either the birds or the animals in the woods. The usual performances were gone through here in the usual way. An agonizing screech at intervals broke the sylvan utopianism as intimated by the gentle cooing of the dove: but I could never be sure whether the cry was of death or love, pain or pleasure. The sudden loud flapping of unseen wings within the shades often startled me. The cuckoo made its appearance in due course, uttering its throaty gurgle while on the wing, and its famous announcement when in the tree. Occasionally a crow flew across, not as the crow is supposed to fly, but with sudden slight turnings and sharp hesitations as if it had remembered something too late. Sometimes, though very seldom, a peewit appeared, lover not of the woods but of the field and the wide desolate place dedicated to history and slow time, into which that plaintive cry, those mournful numbers, flow and melt away.

The birds which most often – late in the year – provided me with entertainment were the starlings. An immense force had taken up residence quite close, and towards evening they carried out extensive manoeuvres. Suddenly I would hear a noise from above as if a gale were blowing up, and I would see a black cloud moving much faster than a cloud; and as it moved, this composition of birds closed to the size of a football, then opened in the shape of a fan, closed again and now became a snake a hundred yards long twirling about in the air, then a carpet being shaken by invisible hands – each transformation being carried out with great celerity. Every bird went perfectly in wing with all the rest, so that however much the gathering twisted and turned it looked more like a single strange creature than a company – the few stragglers like feathers that had been blown off the body owing to the violence of the movement. What the purpose of all these operations was, I don't know. It gave all the appearance of being without utilitarian motive, and is, ten to one, pure *joie de vivre*, play, art for art's sake.

As for animals, I very often heard a sudden nervous chortle followed by a scampering noise, and looking up saw a red or grey squirrel, the creature that always delights us by the beauty of its tail and the strength of those paws that turn the perpendicular into the flat. Immediately my dog would bark, and it would dash higher up. Yet its behaviour was curious. It was as safe as a church in those branches; but it didn't think so, and leapt frantically from tree to tree, accomplishing jumps which made me nervous, and then coming to a very wide jump, failed to make it, landed on the ground uninjured, and scuttled into the undergrowth. It could have remained at ease in the first tree it went up. The species to which it belongs has had centuries behind it of practising in thus escaping from the earthbound beasts. Why has it not learnt to stay put in the security of the lofty boughs? Why does it lose its head?

The deer had more sense in using their legs. There were quite a few of these wonderful animals in the Chase, and the barks of the trees had suffered accordingly, for deer have a partiality for the barks of young trees. I did not see very many. Occasionally when I was making no noise, one appeared and came quite close. If I remained silent and absolutely still it did not observe me. For animals do not see with their eyes. Not that they are blind, it is that objects are not individually separated by a governing intelligence. This extraordinary fact has saved many a man's life in the jungle, and made close observation of animals possible for the naturalist. Then if I stepped on a breaking twig or deliberately clapped my hands it would leap away through the wood with that aristocracy of speed and grace that makes these creatures the queens of the forest. On an early morning in the half-light at a particularly lonely part of the Chase I saw a whole drove of them, and on another occasion at the same hour my dog gave chase to a solitary deer. It stopped and gave battle, and to my astonishment it looked as if my dog was getting the best of it. I called him off. Afterwards I was sorry that I had done so, for I might have witnessed a truly jungle scene.

Some animals alarmed me rather than I them. The tiny weasel pursuing a large rabbit mesmerized to a slow wobbling gait, is a sight most monstrous and intimidating. Indeed, weasels almost paralyse me. Once I sat at a place where three holes abutted a few feet distance from each other. When I sat down there a weasel looked out of one of the holes and spat at me as if delivering a curse, then retired only to appear immediately at the next hole to hiss at me again, after which it drew back its head and shot it out again at the third hole to curse me from that angle. This performance went on for some time: I had to keep turning my head first one way then another as each second the ferocious face looked out of a hole to glare and spit and curse. It seemed to be charged with such potency that I really wouldn't be surprised if I saw a weasel pursuing an elephant paralysed with fear.

Another creature that alarmed me was the adder. Now and then I came upon the reptile, even two or three together. In grey scales or in chequered green. Finding one of considerable size, I toed it, and it rushed away through the privet's undergrowth at extraordinary speed. It didn't crawl, squirm, or hunch its way forward; but *glided* along – as astonishing as if you saw a boat dash through the water without oars or screw. I caught it up in my hand by its middle. It turned its visored head round, opened its trap-door of a mouth, and stuck its barbed fang deep into my thick leather glove (which I had carefully slipped on). Once, twice, three times it struck, then gave up and simply kept darting in and out of its mouth that long terrible tongue, shaped at the end like a tiny anchor or arrow-head. Now and then it gave great wrenches with its whole body to escape my grasp. But I held it firmly and gazed steadfastly into its primeval countenance. It is remarkable how utterly baffling such a creature is. One gazes, one tries to concentrate but somehow one cannot *take it in*. One can hold a conversation with a dog; one could almost shake a horse by the hoof; many a sow is as human to look at as a Victorian lady being amused; a cow often reminds us of some friends; a lamb might be a baby; the birds, like many of us, are vocalists; the monkey shares our secret. But the reptile – I'm afraid no communication is possible. However, I put this one down to pursue its destiny without further hindrance from me, as I felt it had the right to do.

I shall not add much more to my list, but I loved the owl because of its astonishing silence and lightness of touch; I admired the nightjar which was like an alarmclock which couldn't stop; and it would be wrong to forget the pheasant, little pleasure as that poor lumbering bird gives us. Every time I approached the wood it startled me by suddenly springing out of some hidden place on my path with its appalling rattle of a screech and made its straight, blundering, joyless flight away through the wood. That jarring sound is the nearest thing in Nature to something mechanical – as if a machine had been made by mistake. Which reminds me that there is one more animal entitled to a place here. Opposite my wood there was another one belonging to another estate, and rising on a slope so that I commanded a clear view of it. At a given time of the year the partridge and pheasant sportsmen appeared. As they beat their way along through the wood they uttered noises which brought them into such close relation to the brute creation that it is proper to include them here in this short account of animal life found in the woods from time to time.

13 *The Old Woodman*

During some of the summer a woodman and his grandson came from an adjoining estate to make hurdles out of the hazel which I had cut down. And at last, at long last, I came upon the countryman of tradition, the countryman celebrated in books, but who can now only be found in odd corners. He was not a Hardy 'character', nor a Wordsworthian 'leech-gatherer'. Not an 'amusing' man, nor quaint, nor given to making 'wise' remarks culled from his years, nor in command of a picturesque phrase. Such men can be found in Ireland, and probably in Scotland and Wales. The English equivalent possesses no playboy characteristics, nor love of generalization, nor much sense of humour, nor desire to make an effect; but he is so completely sincere that any remark he does make has the advantage of being genuine.

He belonged to the generation that had started work sixty-odd years ago at the age of eleven, beginning then to make spar-gads and hurdles such as he is still making now. The passage of years might be written in financial terms: today spar-gads are thirty-five shillings a thousand as against eight shillings a thousand in the old days. Today a man can make £1 per thousand spars while in the former era he got 2s. 6d. – his wages then in the ordinary way being 10s. a week as opposed to the £4 of today. Thus a man of that kind will have seen some material changes.

Though he was well into the seventies he did not show many signs of being an old man, age had not wearied him; the expression on his face had no sourness in it whatever; his manner of addressing his grandson was extremely pleasant; and he seemed to get on wholly without swearing. He was not a talker, but he enjoyed talking on general topics, and took your point at once (if you did not exaggerate).

He showed me how to make hurdles and spar-gads, and how to loop together the bundles – this last being almost as elaborate a process as hurdle-making itself. He himself had dealt with this wood eighteen years previously, and obliquely I tried to find out his opinion of my thinning and axe-work. He found no fault with it, in fact praised it. In another man I would probably have taken this for politeness; but I thought he really did mean it, and this gave me no small pleasure.

One day, after he had given me the figures regarding the spar-gads, I asked whether he thought the labourers were happier today. He replied firmly and without hesitation – 'No, they are not.' He said they were not satisfied, and were less happy. He went on to say how he used to do general farm-work during the summer months and then return to the wood. He emphasized what a good time haymaking was in those days. Everyone turned out, whole families, having great tea-parties in the field: it was something everyone looked forward to, including the children. No one had to work at a desperate pace, for there were so many workers; and since there were so many workers the job was done quite as quickly as at the present day.

Such are the imponderables of progress. More wages, less jolliness, and the machines not making for less hard work but for fewer workers. The goal of life, judging by our actions, is efficiency. It is really happiness. And the great snag is that neither machines nor £.s.d. seem able to open that door.

In the old days if the agricultural labourer was not religious he was at any rate superstitious. The super-stitious man is profounder than the blasé sceptic, for he is at least *aware* of the 'mystery', and it is one of the little ironies of life that the latter imagines himself superior. Today the attendance at a village church is often only three. For the most part people simply do what is 'done', regardless of conviction. In the old days it was not done not to go to church. Today it is hardly done to go. There is no superstition, and the attitude towards religion is one of indifference at best, and at worst, and more often, of undisguised derision. Hence – quite apart from *believing* this or that – the whole background of word-music from the Bible with its accompanying attitude of reverence and its sanctification of joy and sorrow, no longer informs the life of the people.

The old woodman did not belong to the generation that had lost these good things, and I knew it was safe to make a remark to him concerning the anti-religious trend of workers in general today. It pleased him, for presently he came out with a generalization of his own without any prompting from me. He glanced round the wood, and slowly and haltingly choosing his words, said: 'If I do say to a farmer now, Look how they plants do grow; look at thik field or yourn and see how they do grow without help; there must be a wonderful God behind they plants – he would not understand I.'

'No,' I replied, 'he would probably say that his overhead charges had been very heavy this year, and that he was not going to make nothing out of it, not a penny.'

'That's just what he would say,' affirmed the old man.

And I told him how the foreman had looked over the wood and declared – 'It's only dead money.'

'Oo ah!' said the old man, 'that's the way it is now. That's the way it is.'

Not more than a month or two had passed before he and his grandson had constructed about £40 worth of hurdles. There was something extraordinarily satisfactory about the rows of them leaning neatly one against another, or staked flat ten or more feet high – all twisted by the finger of man out of the hazel bushes, while those same bushes were engaged in sending forth new shoots for future hurdles.

It was interesting to notice how woodmen, working within a given radius for a fair length of time, generally build a comfortable shelter for themselves, against weather and as a dining-room. A few pieces of corrugated tin, two or three poles, and some straw sheaves make an excellent little room to retire into when it pours, and a cloak-room and bicycle-shed at all times. Outside the

shelter, on raw winter days, a fire is lit and kept going –
very pleasant at meal times. In this, as in some other
respects, the woodman has the advantage over other
workmen on the land. I have yet to meet the woodman
willing to change his job for any other department or
agricultural activity.

One day I asked the old man – 'Do you ever wish that
you had done anything else in life, been anything else?'
He did not need to pause and think over his answer, and
then perhaps give a non-committal one. 'No,' he said
firmly, 'I do not, and the longer I live the more sure
I am of that.'

At last I stood beside a contented man, one with many
years upon his back, who did not feel that others had
got a fairer deal out of life; who was not greedy for
position, nor envious of riches, nor indifferent to the
beauty that is freely given to the poor in places such
as this.

I had noticed that he sometimes lay down and took a
nap after dinner, and I mentioned how delightful it was
to lie down and sleep in the wood. He agreed with me.
'It's as if thik birds do watch e,' he said, 'and thik trees
do bend over e.'

14 *A Way of Living*

One of the great advantages of a woodman's job is that
in his old age if he wishes to retire on his pension, he
can at the same time supplement it by peaceful and
easy-going piece-work. Just such an old man came to the

woods from time to time to make stakes and faggots out of my drifts. He took it easy, arriving sometimes before ten and going home at about four. This filled in his day beautifully. If it came on wet he was none too pleased for 'it don't do,' he said, 'to get back too early'. But he wasn't in the least anxious about the money element. His simple needs were perfectly well met by his pension and what he made in the wood, and his days were filled pleasantly. He had a very nice cottage down in the village, free. So had the other old woodman, a delightfully placed and good cottage – for there is no sense in supposing that the countryman is always or even usually badly off in this matter as against the townsman. (And the man who talks about 'the disgraceful housing conditions of rural England' should go and have a look at an Irish village!)

Anyway, in the sphere, I found happy and contented men. Modern life is a labyrinth in which most men are lost. To find a way, a path is not easy. They had found one. Nothing elaborate about it; not the way of the Cross; not the Eightfold Path; but the way of the peasant whose *wants* are few. This gets them through, and I often think of them, I shall always think of them, as men who having escaped from all the escapisms of the modern world, were at peace. I used to visualize them sometimes when, on visits to London, I found myself again in the bus or under the ground. And when I got back amongst the trees again I would feel the full force of the farce of modern civilization; I would see with the clear vision of hatred the foul torrent of respectable insanity that makes the majority of men inferior to monkeys, and their works in thousands and thousands of cases absurd beyond the conception of any savage.

There were times when, sitting under the oak tree in the early morning, I felt that so much was here given that if all the millionaires of all the world came ready to do my bidding and answer my Go here or Go there, I would have nothing to say except Go away. I was in a position to use my body for a period and then my head and pen. Could I ask more than this? or seeking, find? The Rights of Man are all very well, but we shall save the social world only when we pay attention to the *needs* of men. To do hard agricultural work half the day and hard cultural work the other half – that for many would answer their psychological needs. But no effort is made to make that kind of thing possible. We imagine that everything will be all right if we all produce as many objects as possible and distribute them to everybody. We refuse to think of man's Needs and go on and on thinking only of his Rights and his Pay. Never about his psychological and physiological needs – nay, never!

I could satisfy this need here, but only on condition that the whole of Europe, the whole of North America and Canada, the British Empire, Russia, China, and Japan could be engaged in warfare instead of welfare – myself only having to attend Home Guard. But there it was, I was able to do it. And I shall not easily forget, even when the frost of age is on my head, how after a few hours' work in the morning, I had earned enough to pay my rent, and in the afternoon the grocery bill. That is something that I shall never forget! And so, for a moment adopting the role of the wise councillor, I would say to any young man, or young man and woman, ambitious only for peace and sanity – Learn the craft of Forestry, enter the woods, and happiness may yet be yours.

15 *Different Moods in the Wood*

I can offer the above small piece of advice to anyone likely to be glad of it with a clear conscience, because any woodmen I have known always seemed to be doing well and were satisfied. But, speaking very personally, given the choice between permanent agricultural work of a general nature and forestry, I would not choose forestry – though doubtless I would often long to get back to the woods again. In this account I celebrate the pleasures of working in the wood, indeed I sing its joys. But too much hangs on the weather and the time of year. Long hours in a wood during wet or dark or heavy days, can be most melancholy. One can be elated amongst trees, even inspired again and again, in conditions such as I have already rehearsed. It is also possible, and indeed a frequent experience, to be numbed by trees. On dreary, drizzly days I often became stupefied and paralysed in mind as well as weary and lifeless in body.

I have always loved to have a View. The mountains and the sea appeal to me so strongly that I do not dare to think about them nor to mark the absence in England, save in the north, of the glen, the real glen through which the river roars. Thus I'm afraid that I am quite capable of feeling too enclosed working for long periods in an English wood. I love a view, I say, even from the field on the highest part of a farm, and to plough such a field is better than any work in the wood. Sometimes when I walked through the Chase beyond my fence, wandering along, getting lost even and wondering where I had got to, and suddenly came upon a gate leading into a cornfield washing knee-deep against the cliff of trees, I felt a great nostalgia for open spaces and clear views and the turned furrow and the glorious plough.

Thus my moods would go up and down, and as I have no axe to grind save my steel one, but only truth to tell, I shall not pretend that as a woodman I could ever be wholly satisfied. My spirits were very much influenced by the weather. In the fields, the cold, the dark, the dreary, or even the wet days make much less difference, sometimes none at all, sometimes a pleasant change. But the change from sunlight to a drizzle in the wood is a very definite thing, and makes its full effect. The kingdom of heaven is within you, it is said. No doubt there is great truth in that. But an honest man must acknowledge how often his interior is dictated by the exterior scene. Sometimes I have almost felt my heart *contract* at the sudden coming on of a cold darkness, and expand at the smiling beams swiftly pervading the weary, dripping scene around.

During March, April, and May the wood is the place. The sleeping trees awake. At their feet the flowers rise up and we gaze at them with absurd surprise. The birds declaim rather than sing. We stand in the midst of rejoicing life. By June the more obvious flowers have completed their act, they have had *their* summer, their autumn, and now are in their winter of desolation.

Others are taking their place – the rock-rose, the herb-willow, the garlic, the foxglove – but the abundance has gone, and the colour blue, so rich, so varied, is seen no more save in the sky. We have become accustomed to the green of the trees. The birds are reticent.

In July a hush falls upon everything. The silence is disquieting. The silence of a wood at all times is something to reckon with; it seems to pervade one's personality, and I seldom open my lips even to speak to my dog. In July it is a principality. In such an atmosphere ambition wilts, mental strife seems futile, the arts unreal. Filled with unease, one would gladly leave the silent and too solemn trees for a more human scene.

For a more deadly silence go to a pine wood. One day in June when I had wandered farther into the Chase I came to a pine plantation. I stepped out of the privet-choked pathway into its darkness. I walked there without making the slightest noise, for there is no floor, no man-made carpet so soft and yielding to the tread as these massed needles. There was not a speck of green on this ground. I felt awe in the silence. No bird sang, nor wing flapped, nor rabbit scuttled, nor stick cracked. I was enclosed and submerged in a silence like a substance. It was broken occasionally by a squall of wind heard above in the branches of the pines, that wild, watery, bare-beached, oceanic sound that even at the height of summer has no summer in it, and beats against the heart and calls to mind man's endless tale of tempest and of wrong.

Standing there in the darkness of this fir wood, I looked towards the edge and saw the greenery beyond.

It had become a bright green light and I thought the sun must have come out. Yet the sun had not come out, the sky was very cloudy. But from in there that undergrowth immediately outside did shine strongly like a green light. Also in the middle of this plantation there was a pool of green – owing to a break in the trees. Where the light could penetrate, the green had formed – chiefly moss and dog's mercury, a little pool that stopped immediately at the end of the open space.

I was hardly wrong, I reflected, in imagining that I was looking out upon green lights. For that is what I was looking at. The light from heaven shone upon the ground and the plants received it, and – by virtue of chlorophyll, we say – turned it into green substance. That undergrowth is light made visible: it is light made tangible.

Cheered by the thought of this radiant miracle, I emerged from the shade of the sombre aisles and pushed my way home through the tangible pieces of sunshine that blocked my path.

16 *The Scavengers of Corruption*

One day in July I was cutting down a very large and thick-stemmed hazel bush. It had been left alone for so many years that the stool was full of holes and cups and soft, dry-leaved hiding-places. I had cut away about a dozen of the branches and had lifted my axe to strike another, when my eye was caught by something in one of those recesses of the stool. Five small yellow flowers, fresh and strange, stood erect amidst a little bed of dry leaves. They quivered as if blown gently by a breeze. But there was no breeze: and looking closer I saw that they were not flowers; they were five wide open beaks of new-born birds.

Abandoning my axe I knelt down and peered into this nest thus placed so low. The beaks closed and I saw simply the creatures, sightless, no eyes yet opened, no feathers to cover them save here and there a patch of furry stuff on the red flesh. They could not see but they could hear, and when I made a noise all the beaks opened wide again, quivering and giving the impression that they were really shouting an appeal for food, though their voices could not reach me. Then their beaks closed and the pitiful, hideous little bodies sank down into the nest once more. Pathetic beyond measure. Fatally forced into Being. Trembling symbols of the sheer affliction of life, the pure burden of birth.

Those open beaks had looked like flowers for a moment. Yet how different is a flower from an animal in the matter of food. The beaks shouted in mute agonizing appeal for one thing only – the death of another that they might live. Here in this tiny nook in England, as in the roughest jungles of the world, the Law must be fulfilled – thy life or my life. No doubt this proves that death is nothing to worry about and that we are all members of one another in the completest sense; nevertheless man turns away from the animals and from himself and gazes with relief upon the trees and the flowers. They are alive. They multiply in numbers, they increase in strength. Yet, though they may struggle together for light, they never hunt, never prey upon others, never eat themselves. Alive, radiant, yet free from our Order and our Law – eating only the air, only the earth.

I left the stool of this hazel without cutting any more branches, so that the birds might rest in peace. When I went again I saw a robin feeding them with a worm – though I couldn't get close enough to see what her scheme of distribution was amongst five. So they were evidently young robins, born at this strange hour of late July. But next time I came the nest was empty. The chicks had gone and did not return. Their home had been opened by me to the dangers of the wood, and so no doubt, before their time, they had perished that some other creature might not perish.

On my way home I picked up a dead bird. Having just gazed into the cradle of life, I felt a desire to take home the dead body and watch with like attention the activities of this poor discarded garment that was now the cloth of death. I put it in a basin and left it in a shed. Returning after a week, I found it had come to life again. It was breathing heavily. Its tongue popped in and out of its beak, its eyes flashed, and it made a grinding noise. This surprised me; but I then saw that the tongue was really a white worm, the flashing eye a white worm, while the body heaved owing to the squirming activity of the pack of worms inside the corpse.

To find the explanation of this we need go no farther than the female bluebottle on the point of laying her eggs. She prefers to lay them in meat, in a hole in the meat, which will serve as cradle and as food. For this purpose she finds nothing so good as dead birds. The procedure is as follows. She approaches the corpse and makes straight for the beak. If it is tightly closed she will go to the eye-sockets, but if it is open she thrusts her egg-conducting tube, her oviduct, into the hole and proceeds to lay her eggs, an operation which, allowing for rests from labour, may take two hours – after which she goes away and dies. The bird's beak has now been packed pretty full, the tongue and throat being white with layers of eggs. Here they remain for two days, after which time they are transformed into maggots, who then descend down the throat of the bird.

I made my examination several days after they had gone down there and had been composing themselves while decomposing the bird. Indeed they had so completely taken possession that the whole body heaved about, and some of these white, squirming maggots, like small spaghetti, had returned to the throat and also entered the eye-sockets. Already the body had lost much of its weight, for death is heavy and life is light.

I opened the flesh a bit more so that I might observe the main work of reconstruction. I gazed down at the living tubes as they squirmed and twisted and turned and turned them at their task, building up new life in the abominable ferment of corruption. The bluebottle is necessary. The bluebottle is good. All things in Nature have a meaning and a purpose. All are necessary. All are right. If it were not so, if any one thing were wrong, then nothing could be right; if a single error marred the scheme then we could count on nothing, all would be lost, we could hope for nothing, there would be nothing for it, as Edward Carpenter said, 'but to fold our hands and be damned everlastingly'. But since it is not so we can afford to face the facts. It is expedient, on occasion, to gaze down into the pit as well as up towards heaven, to look at the roots of Nature as well as at her flags, regarding the burden of the beginning and the dereliction of the end alike without flinching, so that from time to time the seeing eye, the accepting mind, may receive the vision of what some men call beauty and others truth.

17 The Growth of Trees

I carried out my work of thinning on the basis of 'cuts' measuring twenty feet. Each of these slices went from one end of the wood to the other – a question of several hundred yards. The portion done presented a great transformation: from the side you could easily see through it till the eye hit the dark wall of trees and undergrowth not yet touched. When I had finished one cut and then went back and started again at a new one, so much time had often elapsed that shoots had already begun to grow from the stumps of the trees I had cut down earlier. The rapidity of their growth almost reminded me of bracken.

Looking at such shoots one might think that a tree is only a kind of big flower. But the most striking thing about a tree is that it remains standing. It does not collapse after a season. The flowers fall down every year: their trunks (or stalks) give way, and a whole new plant must take the place of the old. The tree-trunk does not fall down and start again; it bequeaths one year's work in the form of a monument, and next year builds another storey on top of it. It lays foundation-stones called buds that grow into branches. And as it builds its head out of the air of heaven, as it opens its leaves, as it spreads its branches, the prop upon which it rests, its trunk, increases in strength and girth. It increases thus because every leaf connects itself with the soil by sending down a cable. Trees have been called *collective beings*: and truly we may think of each leaf as an individual plant with a separate stem joining it with the earth. This connecting link is at the same time a tax which each leaf pays to the whole, it is a tribute levied for its upkeep. Every new leaf on the great tree in the forest lowers down this cable, this silken thread, this fibre, this cord, until reaching beneath the surface of the earth it becomes a root – and the sum of these connecting wires increases the girth of the tree every year. A tree-trunk is really a mass of wood-covered waterways linking leaf with root, ever widening as the building grows from above. We see here a wonderful natural example of two offices being performed by a single operation. The leaves require extra sustenance from the earth, and having received it they reach out ever higher and bulkier into the air; but this increase does not break down the spray, the branch, or the stem, because of the tribute, the wood-tax that has been paid, in virtue of which the spray, the branch, and the stem become proportionally larger and stronger. That is how every tree makes its trunk. Every leaf of every tree has sent down a tiny string, covering and clinging to the shoot beneath, and increasing its thickness. Singly it may seem a slender offering, but not in its hardened multiplicity. By itself it might not appear to be equal to its great task or certain of reaching its goal; but softness is often the sign of strength and determination. Just as granite rocks will be worn away under the washing of the softer substance of waves, and water itself fail to impress the greater softness of the flowering polyps that build up the coral reefs, so this law of humble power can be seen in the flowing downwards of the wooden threads. 'Each according to his size and strength, wove his little strand of cable, as a spider his thread,' wrote Ruskin in this connection, 'and cast it down the side of the springing tower by a marvellous magic – irresistible! The fall of a granite pyramid from an Alp may perhaps be stayed: the descending force of that silver thread shall not be stayed. It will split the rocks themselves at its roots, if need be, rather than fail in its work.'

Two interesting things follow from this. The first is that though a tree may be said to reach maturity in the eye of the timber-merchant, there can never come a time when it ceases to grow. A tree is not like an animal which grows to a certain size, then stops growing and eats only to live instead of to live and to grow. An animal does not build itself by eating through its limbs any more than a man through the tips of his fingers; it does not continually create a head any more than a man grows his head with his hair – it starts with a head. A tree starts without a head. Since it advances upwards by means of a self-building crown, and since every leaf thereof drops an anchor down beneath the surface of the soil, then so long as new leaves appear a greater bulk of crown and width of trunk must follow. But in proportion to the size of the tree will be the rate of growth. I have just mentioned how here in my wood I see several feet of new stems spring up in a few months. The process must inevitably get slower and slower as the ground to be covered by the communicating wires of wood increases. Were I to sit beneath the melancholy boughs of a six-thousand-years-old tree and attempt to note a season's difference, I fear I should not succeed in convincing myself that it had changed at all.

Six thousand years old? Yes, for this brings me to the second thing that follows upon the construction of a tree. Theoretically it need never die. Consider what a tree is – or any plant for that matter. It is not a single being, not one person, as it were (though it may have great personality). It is a group of beings. Looking at a hive, we should be tempted to say – Here are many units, yet it may really be a multiplicity of units. If we examine the little creature called the hydra, found in stagnant ponds, we find that its manner of giving birth to new hydras is by growing them upon its person like buds on a tree. All of them feed from the communal stomach; but after a certain period they break off from their parent to live a life of independence. When we examine a coral reef we find that it consists of polyps. A polyp has the same organization as a hydra, the same method of budding its offspring – with one difference. The hydra breaks off from the parent body, the polyp continues to remain attached. But it proceeds in the same way as the hydra, each polyp budding its children rather than lying or delivering them, and they all feed from the communal sac, the continual growth of which means the spreading out and up of their domicile, their polypary. This polyp, or 'coral insect', is a little hollow globule of gelatinous matter, a tiny sac whose mouth is bordered by eight leaf-shaped appendages, fringed at the edges: eight tentacles opening like the petals of a flower. No wonder a coral looks like a rock covered with brilliant flowers. What is that rock made of? How did these flower-like animals called polyps come to have this pedestal? Because it is made of their own exudations. They exude stone. With their own excrement they build up and rest upon a monument as hard as marble. The whole reef is made of polyp. The softest of all creatures has turned into the hardest of all rocks. These reefs continue to grow by means of the collective effort of millions upon milliards of polyps, so that an archipelago such as the Maldive in the Indian Ocean can comprise no less than twelve thousand reefs, and a reef can spread over an area of thirty-three thousand miles. No term needs to be set to the life of a polypary since it is a collection of beings continuously giving birth to others by process of budding, and continuously bequeathing their excrement to the magnificent ocean-dunghill upon which they stand.

All life is related by the work of the twin sisters Time and Motion – often called Evolution – and it is not hard to see how similar is the growth of a plant to the growth of a coral reef. We can see that a tree is a community of beings rather than an individual. You cannot cut limbs off an individual and expect it to live, or the limb itself to live. That is exactly what we can do with a tree. If we want a fresh tree it is sufficient to cut off a living branch and plant it. It will spread roots and grow, while the parent will not suffer. We can even plant the young branches of one tree on to another tree, which we call grafting, an operation which explains the justice of Dupont de Nemours' definition – 'A plant is a family, a republic, a sort of living hive, whose inhabitants are fed in the common refectory upon the common stock of food.' This communal stock of food, this sort of omnibus sac, called the trunk, is even ready to feed a species of tree not absolutely fraternal. Figs will not grow on thistles – (though under this ruling one would not be surprised if they did). But Fabre mentions a certain pear tree 'on which, by means of grafting, the whole gamut of cultivated pears was represented. Sweet or sour, dry or juicy, large or small, green or brilliantly coloured, all these pears ripened on the same tree, year after year, always unchanged, faithful to the racial characteristics, not of the tree, their foster-mother, but of the various buds transferred to the common support'. Such an experiment might well have served as proof of the individuality of a bud as opposed to the free association of a tree.

Thus granted, the age of a tree could be very great. In fact if it lives in a spot unexposed to the violence of storm or earthquake and out of the reach of man's commercial activity, it may continue to live for an extra-ordinary period. A good place to find tree-veterans is in the sanctified area of graveyards where, companions of the dead, they are unmolested by the living. Thus in the cemetery of Allouville in Normandy there stands an oak tree some nine hundred years old, whose trunk at ground level shows a circumference of thirty-three feet, while within the aerial forest of its upper branches the cell of an anchorite has been built, and the lower portion of its partly hollow trunk has been used since 1696 as a chapel dedicated to Our Lady of Peace. Many a yew tree in an old churchyard vies in age with the most ancient church, while others look back to times long before any temple was built in the name of Christ. There was a yew tree at Fortingal in Scotland whose concentric rings amounted to two thousand five hundred, and another at Brabourne in Kent whose age was thirty centuries. Oak trees often stand sturdily against the blasts of time. In 1824, a wood-cutter in the Ardennes, on felling a giant of this species, found fragments of sacrificial urns and ancient medals within its trunk, thus connecting it with the barbarian invasions of Europe. It showed no more signs of failing health than the walnut tree noticed by the soldiers of Balaclava in the Crimea, which, though two thousand years old, yielded an annual crop of 10,000 walnuts, the harvesting of which was shared by five families.

The size of such trees can best be imagined when we learn that on the occasion of a giant conifer which once stood on the slopes of the Sierra Nevada in California, falling before the axe, the woodmen had to use a long ladder even to mount its prostrate trunk, as if scaling the roof of a house. The bark of this tree was removed in a single piece from the length of twenty-two feet, which served to enclose a room in which one hundred and forty children could play hunt-the-slipper. This giant displayed three thousand concentric layers of wood, showing that it reached back to the time when, according to tradition, 'Samson released in the cornfields of the Philistines, foxes, to whose tails incendiary torches were attached.' These conifers of the Sierra Nevada had grown to three hundred feet or more. Other veterans have expressed themselves more in their crowns, like that yew tree in the cemetery of Haie-de-Routot which in 1832 spread its foliage over the entire churchyard and part of the church itself. I have already mentioned the Chestnut Tree of the Hundred Horses at Etna, under the cover of which the Queen of Aragon found room for her whole retinue; but in Mexico there is a cypress contemporary with Noah, standing in the cemetery of Santa Maria de Fesla near Oaxaca, beneath whose boughs Cortez, the conqueror of Mexico, found room to shelter his army. The crown of the baobab tree at Senegambia near Cape Verde, is even more remarkable. The diameter of the trunk is greater than the height of the tree, the latter being but fifteen feet and the former thirty! – a column fit to support the mighty dome which is two hundred feet in diameter. This baobab tree is a worthy companion in distinction with the dragon tree of Orotova in the Canary islands whose trunk cannot be encircled by ten men holding hands. Both trees, older than the Pyramids, hold the memory of six thousand years, and show every promise of ignoring the terms of Time.

18 The Feeling Intellect

On sultry summer days it was interesting to observe the insectitude activity. Before the temperature rose the air would be moderately clear, but when the sun came out into the heavy, windless, sultry atmosphere then swarms of insects, especially a certain kind of fly, rising from nowhere particular, began to buzz round and round madly as if at that moment created, released, unloosened from a melting solid.

A massive, solid unity – that's the impression one often gets of the earth; almost motionless and asleep at the freezing Poles, partially melted into bits at these climes, and in the Tropics, under the equatorial rays, melted out into a seething flow and flood of fast-moving particles in every shape and size.

Why does life hang together so well, seeing that everything is at everything else's throat? Presumably because it is not really in parts. It is not a question of parts that make a whole but of a whole presenting itself in parts. If this were not so, the parts would certainly not hang together, they would hang separately as it were. The unity is so obvious that it would hardly seem worth mentioning; yet I cannot feel any confidence that the reader will regard it as a platitude. Certainly our *working-habit* of thought is not unity, not synthesis; it is almost always in terms of disunity, which, so far from being regretted has been conceived as excellent, as a triumph meriting the title of 'victorious analysis'. The results are not wholly good. We can do wonders with the inorganic – there we are victorious, able to create a thing like the gramophone no less than other mechanical constructions, not all of which are beautiful or of good report. But in the field of medicine (not surgery), of religion, of philosophy, of economics and politics, we are nearly lost – because we cannot yet think in terms of the unity. (We do better in the field of agriculture, because we have to act in terms of unity or perish.)

I enter thoughts of this kind in this account because they arise when I am confronted with Nature. If thoughts are simple experience arising from common sensation, they are sometimes worth putting down. I hope I have Reason on my page. But not ratiocination, not thinking before I experience. It is Wordsworth's *'feeling* intellect' that holds interest for me. The old adage 'I think, therefore I am' is less helpful than the other way round, 'I am', that is 'I experience, therefore I think.' Wordsworth held that ecstasy is the highest form of thought, since it is the nearest we get to *communication* with truth. And after a visitation of ecstasy caused in him by the earthly spectacle, he said – 'Thought was not, *in enjoyment it expired.'*

If it be complained that on this showing our systems simply follow our feelings I see no harm in it. Sensation is not so very eccentric. We back each other up. Anyway, to think without the thought springing from felt experience cannot but be as void as merely second-hand thinking – with which anyone could fill a book, and which is as valueless as second-hand observation. During the daily intercourse of life we need second-hand thinking all the time, but if we do not experience our own philosophy and religion we have none. And if we write it down we do not expect to be able to hand it to anyone else. This kind of knowledge 'cannot be handed from one person having it to another person not having it', as Whitman said. But we can support the findings of others, and stimulate experience-knowledge.

The love of Nature is deep in England. And I think that what is behind this love is the instinct that Nature has a secret for us, and answers our questions. Take that foxglove over there – for we have now reached August in this chronicle. It stands singly where there had been such a wonderful display of bluebells that it then looked as if a section of the sky had been established upon earth (though not really the same colour at all!). That foxglove with its series of petal-made thimbles held up for sale to the bees, puts me at ease upon the subject of – progress. It is quite obvious that the foxglove cannot be *improved*. There is no progressing beyond that point for that particular Appearance. There is no room for improvement in the bluebell nor in any of the other exhibits. The fact is we get perfection in this form and in that form. Hence Shakespeare's 'ripeness is all', and Tennyson's 'God fulfils Himself in many ways', and Whitman's 'there can never be any more perfection than there is now', and Heraclitus' 'Life is a Fountain of Fire, an ever-living Flame, kindled in due measure, and in like measure extinguished'. Evolution is not something going up and up and up – but a series of perfect Forms. The goal of each Form is the fulfilment of its own unique perfection. There is no point in our gazing raptly into the future for paradise if it is at our feet.

But this is not true of Man, you say. That is the paradox. In a perfect world he is imperfect. But then he has attained a new thing of his own – consciousness. Complete consciousness will be his ripeness, his perfection. That will probably take time, say several million years. But why worry? There might be five million years after that of perfect humanity. Meanwhile our foxglove can keep us sane at least about subjects such as beauty and art. There is no steady evolutionary 'progress' in these things, only different expressions. Just as there will never be a better foxglove so there will never be a better Shakespeare.

Near the foxglove are the bluebells. They have now dried into seeds. Every stalk is hung with a rattling belfry of seed pouches. These once green stalks are now dry, yellow, and very light. Each bell is a hard, closed pouch of seed. I pluck a whole stalk and open one of the pouches. I find an average of fifty seeds in each, and on each stalk there is an average of eight pouches. $8 \times 50 = 400$. There are ten stalks in every area of, say, my boots' width and length – that is, room for 4,000 seeds. Looking round, one is impressed by the massive number of possible bluebells. It is impossible not to feel the sweep of Nature's vitality. What is plainly seen is not death, but everlasting creation and life. Such a scene is as much revelation as the early garment of blue, it is as truly a sign of goodwill, and has in it as great a promise. There is no need to *reconcile* oneself to the scene. A very small proportion of those seeds will succeed in their struggle for birth, and after birth not all will succeed in getting up. But what of it? It's worth the candle, isn't it? It is better than a *void*, surely. But if the Beginner of life could do what He has done, why could He not have done better, it may be complained; why could He not have eliminated the seamy side? Evidently He couldn't.

19 *Each Its Hour*

In the woods, as elsewhere, it is generally wrong to suppose that we often get the beginning of autumn in September, either in terms of temperature or colouring. I noticed no marked difference in the wood from what it was in the earlier month except that nothing now was due to have its hour. I have often used that phrase to myself, 'have its hour', with regard to woodland scenes; for it is interesting the way in which nearly everything has its particular hour when it, and perhaps it alone, catches the eye of the careless passer-by, though before that time, and again after it, there is nothing strikingly noticeable in that quarter.

Take the elder, for example. There, surely, is a miserable affair; a hopelessly plebeian plant. A bush posing as a tree, a tree failing to be a bush. It is impossible to praise its bark even when healthy, and when in decay it is an inch-thick pole of dirt, the nearest thing to real dirt to be found in Nature. Yet during a few weeks in July the elder has its hour. You actually pause to admire it. For then it is in flower; and those flowers are handed to you on a plate, as it were, or rather they are plates, beautifully decorated with the finest lace, held up before you. The same is true of the hawthorn. During the winter you hardly look at it, not to mention the unfriendly aspect of all armoured trees; but in spring first come the little round white buttons, and then the open flower turning half the tree to white against the blue sky, and giving out that scent which pronounces the spring and comes across to us less like a scent than a memory and a promise of happiness. More spectacular, though less rich, is the hour of that other bush, the blackthorn, which, being neglected through the months, as it were, seizes upon our attention in March by a special act – that of jumping the season of green and going straight to the flower, white first and green second: so that all eyes are drawn towards this one illumination. For at this time there is no green on bush or tree in all the countryside; only the fields are green – and then how lovely they look in their brown and almost black frames! Ah, then it is that the green fields of England shine. All else is dark but they are light. Then suddenly the darkest of all the hedges are lit by artificial snow, the blackthorn becomes the whitethorn, and the poor bush that was so humble is exalted, and its proud peers rebuked.

Speaking as a woodman, I am no friend of the privet; for not only is it very difficult to clean up, but it strays and straddles about without beauty to recommend it; but I am not blind to the fact that in July it also comes into its own and looks positively pretty. Still less do I care for the honeysuckle; but I cannot deny that when those pieces of 'twine' show the green leaf and then the flower, they become the opium of the woods.

Life being what it is, we cannot say that everything has its great hour, though all have their hours of youth, even the evergreens, which though green for ever, put up new leaves every year. And some have two hours: the most striking example being the larch which is seen, when you survey from a rise some stretch of woodland still unleafed, to be the exception – a deep rich meadow-green amidst all the surrounding unopened twigs: and again in autumn it is often so fantastically striking in its decay that that which was dead seems alive again. The imperious hours of the laburnum, lilac, and chestnut need no recommendation from me; but the whitebeam holds our attention almost more than any of the others in spring when the grey sheen of the underleaf shines out, and later when in flower the whole tree is one of the aristocrats of the forest.

Some trees prefer to take their hour in winter. I would put in a claim here for the oak, though possibly its real moment is in spring when in fresh leaf it out-greens everything else – even the beech. But there can be no two opinions that the plane trees come into their own properly in winter when they hold up their little balls before the gaze of the Londoner. And the same is the tale of the elm. It is a question of tracery. The tracery of plane trees and elms is scripture. Could we read that writing, we feel we would have our answer, we would solve our problem, and be shielded from the dark sorrows of our weakness.

It is the elm that knows how to take the sunset better than any other tree. I have been made to pause in my path many a time by elm-tree tracery hung across the dusky winter sky. As I write these words, I recall, so clearly, how having gone up the stairs to the top floor of a high building at Rugby School, I stopped in the passage leading to the classroom. From the window I could see a marvellous sunset behind a line of elm trees. I stood there for some time fixed by the sight. I came in late to that lesson and may have been reprimanded, I don't remember. Nor do I remember the lesson that day, nor the master, though I think it was G F Bradby. But now recalling that hour, I venture to praise the boy, who must have been capable of learning something from the stolen tuition, otherwise he would not have paused to take it. The child is father to the man, we say. Let me then praise my father, even salute him: for he stood there without any ulterior motive, furtively gazing into heaven: he didn't make a song about it, didn't dream of writing it up as a poem to be praised and admired – just stood and gaped!

20 Planting; The Head Woodman; The Fable

During the autumn I did some planting. My thinning process left plenty of room for useful underplanting. There are certain trees which grow best in their early years under shade, and amongst these are beech. Rolf decided to underplant the section of the wood that had been thinned, with beech. There had been a good deal of rain in September and thus the ground was all right for planting in October.

I have just been looking through two forestry manuals to find out what they said regarding Season for Planting. They said nothing. They talked about everything else. So I turned to William Cobbett's manual, not thinking it likely that *he* would let me down. Nor did he. He says with his usual dogmatic clarity – 'If the weather be open and dry, you *may* plant at any time between September and April.' He then goes on to explain which are the very best times. I was interested to note that he says you should not plant in the rain, for I had often heard it so plausibly asserted that it was splendid to plant in the rain, since you are *watering* the roots as you plant. 'A grand day for planting,' said a forester to me one wet afternoon, adding how he had already planted five hundred trees that day. As he happened to be a particularly glib, plausible man, I was not a bit surprised to be faced with a totally opposite school of thought on the subject – 'Never plant in wet weather, nor when *the ground is wet*, if you can possibly avoid it,' says Cobbett again (as you see from the italics). 'The ground never *ought* to be either moved, or walked upon, when it is wet at the top. But we are frequently compelled to do both, or to leave our work wholly undone. It is a very great error to suppose that plants take root quicker for being planted in wet weather. The contrary is the fact. One great thing is, to make the earth that goes close to the roots *fine*; and this you cannot do in wet weather. For this reason it is that I prefer March and April for doing the work of planting: but, be it done at what season of the year it may, the ground ought *not to be wet*; for then it falls in about the roots in lumps, or in a sort of flakes, like mortar. It never gets close and compact about the roots; and if you tread it in it becomes, in dry weather, so hard as to actually pen up the roots of the tree as if they were in a vice.'

We did not plant in the rain, but we did plant in the autumn, for circumstances were such as to permit it, the head woodman being able to come along at that time with two boys and another woodman. This headman,

whose name was Reggie Wyman, was not the same type
as the woodman previously alluded to. He was only
thirty-five, thus belonging to this generation, though not
the last lap of it. If the new generation were composed
of men like him (and there may be many such), then we
need not feel too gloomy about the future. He hadn't
the rather over-serious virtues of the older race, but he
had his own virtues, chief of which was – humanness.
The great thing is to find a human being; that is, a person
capable of friendship and affection, and not submerged
beneath class-consciousness, or envy, or disappointment,
or frustration, or general grudgingness – and possessing
life and inner warmth. We are never markedly success-
ful in our search in any quarter. As the working man
emerged from his long helotism, his attitude towards the
world was inevitably often obstructively self-defensive.
Now it becomes unnecessary, while dignity and pride,
unforced, are often substituted. Reggie was in possession
of inner warmth, and he felt in no sense inferior to
anyone anywhere (but *not* the 'I'm-as-good-as-you' attitude), nor his work of less value and importance to
society than the highest in the land. He was too proud
and too conscious of this; but in him even that was
delightful. For one's attitude towards a man, and his
own attitude towards life for that matter, depends so
much upon his personality – (history is governed nearly
as much by this as by economic factors). Reggie had
considerable personality, and of an attractive kind. Most
working men look older than their arithmetical age. He
looked younger. The most striking attribute of his slight
wiry figure with its good-looking bronzed face, was his

hair – a crop of apparently not-thinning, silky flaxen hair. Always conscious of his appearance, he never wore a hat or cap – again rare amongst working men. He fitted perfectly into the woodland surroundings, as he stood leaning against a tree – he was then the best-dressed man, in his 'shabby' workman's clothes, that I have seen in the course of my life. Realizing this, he frequently draped himself against a tree while gossiping in his high-pitched voice.

He brought with him for this planting, three assistants – an old man and two boys. Boys, as is well known, 'have no character', so one can just say boys and be done with it, recognizing that the word boy denotes life as yet unquenched or tamed; and that the extraneous wrappings of our barbarian modernism, like any other garment, could be exchanged in a twinkling if and when there are leaders of the people ready to introduce new values. Over against these boys was the old man, small, faded, insignificant, and incredibly inoffensive and humble, with nothing to say and hardly ever saying anything – he just wanly smiled amiably.

The method of planting is straightforward enough. You take a spade and thrust it into the soil at a perpendicular angle, and then at right angles to the cut you strike across it: finally dig in again at the foot of the cross, and tilt the spade backwards – and there will be a hole in the centre into which you can place your plant. The main thing is to get it properly in, with its roots spread out and not bunched together – to which end it is good to pull it up a fraction at the last moment while you take away the spade and tread down the earth firmly around the little tree.

Taking a line each, we proceeded to underplant with beech trees a given acreage of the thinned ash wood. Reggie worked by fits and starts, urging the boys forward in his high voice for a period, after which he often paused for a gossip. Keen on music hall, he would outline the merits of various comedians then get down to some more planting before pausing again, to admit, perhaps, that he couldn't do with BBC talks or classical music – which latter he described as 'music which stops and then goes on again'. The Announcers also intrigued him, and he referred to a Yorkshire one who was at that time being tried out, as sounding 'rather common' – though this did not mean that he liked Stuart Hibberd, whom actually he couldn't understand, could not *follow*. Then some more planting followed by a further extension of gossip, this time on the characteristics of a certain fore-man of the estate, who had once, but once only, attempted to interfere in the affairs of the wood, and of that man's 'ignorance' – i.e. manners – when he called at Reggie's house and looked his wife up and down. More planting, and then likely enough a brief outline of the moral life of the village owing to the influx of the military when too many girls became a soldier's relaxation. His tone on most matters was the normal one of cheerful scorn, but on this latter he was rather scandalized, for, though not in the least religious, he was very moral, and a great family man in love with his wife and daughter, proud of the way his daughter had him under her thumb and highly indignant with Beveridge for presuming to extend State Assistance towards her upkeep, for he could look after his own maid, thank you, he didn't want no state assistance for his little maid . . . And thus between our spurts of planting we covered a good deal of ground in conversation. But I write these lines in sadness, for not then did I guess, nor he in any faint way glimpse, the tragedy close ahead that would shatter him.

I do not remember how many trees we planted per day. Not too many I hope – for I want to come and watch this wood from time to time. This is a job which, were I owner, I would not like to have had done in a hurry, and might even feel inclined to praise the man who had planted the least trees per day. Certainly it would be fatal to have it done by piece-workers.

It is said – is it not? – that some men have a special 'touch' when planting, and that the trees put in by them thrive better than others. Hardy represents Giles Winterbourne as such. One enjoys that sort of statement and swallows it. But we may well doubt whether it is really ever actually true. It would be interesting to adopt a severe scientific scepticism towards it and put it to the proof over a given number of acres for a given period of years (that is the scientific method) and see at the end if the magic-touch man really did better than Tom, Dick, and Harry, when they planted properly. Actually I asked the older men whether there was anything in this, and they didn't see what I was getting at. That's always my difficulty – meeting in real life an approximation to fictitious characters. Take another assertion from

The Wood

Thomas Hardy (no man loves re-reading him more than I) when he says of his woodlanders – 'From the light lashing of the twigs upon their faces when brushing through them in the dark, they could pronounce upon the species of the trees whence they stretched; from the quality of the wind's murmur through a bough, they could in like manner name its sort afar off.' I did not strike lucky in coming across woodmen here, old or young, who would answer to that, any more than to Giles' capacity to make a generalization such as 'She's been a bit of a charmer in her time, I believe, a body who has smiled where she has not loved, and loved where she has not married.'

Having planted our acreage, we fenced it in, since everything being food for something else, young barks are much appreciated by rabbits. But our fence was not high enough to keep out deer. I should add here that besides my thinning and planting I carried out systematic pruning over one portion of the wood. There are, of course, two schools of thought concerning the advisability of pruning trees – that is taking away all branches as high as you can reach in order to ensure a straight, thick pole. Since I did prune a portion I shall be able to compare results. Knocking away the rotten lower branches is not the same as pruning and is called 'brashing'. This is a very enjoyable job when dealing with the fir variety of tree, for then a single slash with the back of the bill-hook knocks off a number of branches with a loud bang, and you get a clear space. A few more whacks and you see the straight trunk hitherto completely hidden by the multitude of small branches.

Though I planted, thinned, pruned, and brashed I took no part in the final operation of felling. This takes place when the tree has reached 'maturity'. Sometimes, at this stage trees look so well that owners have felt constrained to leave them standing. This is deplorable. It betrays uncertainty as to the purpose of life, which is commerce. We should always bear in mind the noble words of Mr C E Curtis who in his *Practical Forestry* writes – 'If we visit the woods in any part of the country we see this – (trees which having attained maturity have not been touched) – and with regret, and attribute it either to ignorance or to love of the scenic rather than the commercial aspect of forestry on the part of the landowner.'

Joking apart, if a man does not cut down his trees at the proper time, it really means that he does not take the job seriously. That has been the case in England far too long. People want quick returns, and nothing is less quick than the returns of forestry – though if the whole thing is planned systematically there is a splendid ultimate return and *continuous* takings the whole time on faggots, firewood, stakes, spars, poles, fencing material, shaws, and hurdles. Unfortunately the general attitude towards planting trees is a feeling that only after one is dead will the rewards be coming in. We are reminded of Dr Johnson's saying – 'Most men when exhorted to plant a tree begin *to think of dying.*' They are discouraged by the thought that they shall not live to see the pecuniary profit of their endeavour. A sad reflection, which only serves to make out a case for State Ownership in order to arrest the decay of British Forestry. Yet any man who is in a position to go in for it, is with absolute certainty carrying out noble work, supplying the material for countless things necessary to the life of mankind, work which also has a moral and beautiful aspect. Cobbett, who saw much profit in the business, proving it with facts and figures for his day at any rate, also reminds us of La Fontaine's fable of *The Old Man and The Three Young Men* – 'the wise, the generous, the noble sentiments of which ought to be implanted in every human breast . . . I beg those, who may happen not to understand French, to be pleased to receive, from my pen, the following statement of the mere prosaic meaning of these words, for this absolutely inimitable writer, who, in marks of simplicity the most pleasing that ever followed the movements of a pen, has, on numerous subjects, left, to ages unborn, philosophy the most profound and sentiments the most just and exalted.' After which inimitable introduction Cobbett gives the following translation of La Fontaine's fable.

A man of fourscore was planting trees. 'To *build* might pass; but to *plant* at such an age!' exclaimed THREE YOUNG MEN of the neighbourhood. 'Surely,' said they, 'you are doting; for in God's name, what *reward* can you receive for this, unless you are to live as long as one of the Patriarchs? What good can there be in loading your life with cares about a time you are never destined to see? Pray devote the rest of your life to thoughts on your past errors; give up distant and grand expectations: these become only us YOUNG MEN.' 'They become not even you,' answered the OLD MAN. 'All we do comes late and is quickly gone. The pale hand of fate sports equally with your days and with mine. The shortness of our lives puts us all on a level. Who can say which of us shall last behold the light of heaven? Can any moment of your lives even secure you a second moment? My great-grandchildren will owe shady groves to me: And do you blame me for providing delight for others! Why, the thought of this is, itself, a *reward* which I *already* enjoy; I may enjoy it tomorrow and for some days after that; nay, I may more than once even see the sun rise on your graves.' The OLD MAN was right: one of the three, ambitious to see the New World, was drowned in the port; another pursuing fame in the service of Mars, was suddenly stopped by an unexpected shot; the third fell from a tree, on which he himself was putting a graff: and the OLD MAN, lamenting their sad end, engraved on their tomb the story here related.

21 Experiments and Questions

'Leaf by leaf crumbles the gorgeous year,' wrote the poet. But sometimes the year really *falls*, comes crashing down. Thus here, in November when the leaves were ready to fall but had not done so owing to lack of wind, there suddenly came a tempest lasting a day and a night. Next morning I looked round in vain for leaves still at their stations and saw only one, the terminal leaf on the highest branch of a young hazel bush: just that one, a battered flag that had not fallen. Immediately I stepped into winter.

There are not many beautiful autumn trees, when you come to think of it: not many, I mean, that amaze us like the terrific screens of beech leaves, the bright yellow of chestnut trees, the workmanship put into the evening drapery of the larch and silver birch. These do amaze us however often we see the show; we never look on them with indifference: that the decay of the leaf should be the glory of the leaf, that its day of withering and downfall should rival the beauty of its first unfolding, is a perennial encouragement to all mankind. I do not make any great claim for the ash as a particularly good autumn tree, I think it takes the winter best; but no tree at this time of year displays a more fascinating scheme of seeds – the famous 'bunch of keys', inaptly called.

At this point I must quote Cobbett again (it is always a job to refrain from quoting him if he has touched upon a matter in hand, but I do my best to refrain, recognizing that it is my business unfortunately to give you Collis and not Cobbett). 'If you be curious and have a mind to see a tree in embryo,' he writes, 'take an *ash* seed, put it into a little water lukewarm, and there let it remain for three or four days. Take it out: take a sharp knife, split the seed longways down the middle, and there you will see, standing as upright as a dart, an *ash* tree, with leaves, trunk, and stem, that is to say the head of the root: and all this you will see with the naked eye, as clearly as you ever saw an *ash* tree growing in a field or meadow.'

Being extremely eager to see this I tried the experiment carefully. But I did not see it. I often tried but I never saw the little tree. Using a razor blade I slit the casket that holds the kernel, according to instructions, and I did find something. I found a very neat miniature *spade*. It was exceedingly attractive and surprising to look at, but it was not a tree.

William Cobbett is one of the most convincing writers who ever lived; even when wholly wrong, even when making a prophecy such as that the locust tree will, in fifty years, be the most common in England (owing to his advocacy), even then he is so unqualified in the certitude of his tone that we feel that we *ought* to see locust trees everywhere. And it may be that he was not right in this claim about the embryo *ash* tree. But I am inclined to think that the fault lies with me. This sort of thing, curiously enough, is often a matter of psychology. Experiments *don't work* for me. For other men, or rather for a scientist (who is a special kind of person), the right thing happens at the right time. The great scientist – and of course we are not thinking of anyone like Cobbett – is a man to whom things *occur*. He is not only a man of great research and organization of particulars, he is a man for whom things occur. An example of how they do not occur for me might amuse a reader willing to wander for just a moment away from trees. When wishing to acquaint myself with the life and habits of earthworms, I studied as my chief source of information Charles Darwin's book *The Formation of Vegetable Mould Through the Action of Worms*, published in 1881 by John Murray. Amongst other things, he established by careful experimental proof how the worms manage slowly to bury objects, from stones to cities, if left alone. One day, when strolling in a great Cathedral Cloister, I observed that the grass in the middle contained many flat-slabbed tombstones, some modern, some quite ancient. How interesting, I thought, here I shall be able to see the result of worm-burial before my eyes. I saw a modern stone, 1921, how it was level with the grass, and near it another stone, 1804, which had sunk a considerable distance below the surface. This was excellent. I walked round so that I might see the old tombstones well sunk while the newer ones were still on the surface. I came to Martha Hunt, of Beloved Memory, dated 1870, and then to Nathaniel Groves, Resting in the Lord, dated 1791. But Martha Hunt's tombstone had sunk lower than that of Nathaniel Groves! Trying not to notice this, I passed on and continued to conduct my researches. Some of the other stones conformed to the requirements of the theory, but not all. Coming upon Arthur Mackensie of Beloved Memory, dated 1801, and then upon Elizabeth Wakefield, in Loving Memory of, dated 1910, I was grieved to see that the latter was lower than the former.

I need not say that I do not at all dispute Darwin's findings. Apart from the fact that a hundred reasons could doubtless be given as to why these particular stones were as they were, I feel confident that no fault lay with the worms. It is merely psychologically impossible for things of this kind to turn out well for me. Had Darwin experimented here, we can be sure that the tombstones would have arranged themselves in the proper order. The poet is the man who sees. The philosopher is the man who thinks. The man-of-action is the man who knows what to do. The scientist is the man who discovers. These are special kinds of men, as is soon found by any Tom, Dick, or Harry who assuming the role of one, attempts to see or to think or to lead or to experiment. I fear that I have nothing of the scientist in me, nothing of the naturalist or botanist; I shall never propose a theory supported by experimental proof, I shall never discover anything, never make new things known. I am content to make known things new.

Sometimes I am willing to ask a question. But not often, owing to the difficulty of getting a reply. For instance, I cannot understand why all woods are not found on the highest part of the land. Should not all woods be on hills? It is remarkable what colossal results follow upon minute and slow processes. We see this everywhere, not least in the famous case of the earth-worm; and we might well be pardoned if we failed to believe that the mighty rocks of the early world could ever, by any process however slow, have been changed into soil. Now trees are things which in winter are one size and in summer another size, for they put on clothes called leaves. In the winter a given tree may look quite small – and in the summer enormous. Just outside my window there is a particular example of this, a silver birch. In the winter its marvellous network of twigs gives it a frail look, but when it becomes enleafed the change is remarkable; by midsummer it is a towering substance, a mighty mammoth of a tree standing there in the dusk huge and monumental. In the autumn it does not retain this extra substance, it lets it all fall to the ground. And those leaves do not all evaporate, many of them become vegetable mould. How is it then that after a few years, let alone a few centuries, a forest will not have added enormously to the ground on which it stands? They say that the fungi feed on this decay; but surely not enough.

And the amount in evaporation doesn't seem likely to be equivalent to the deposit, and we cannot say that as much has been taken from the earth in order to make the leaves as is given by their fall, since they take huge supplies also from the air. They weave the atmosphere into visible shape. On a single oak tree seven million leaves have been counted. These leaves hang there throughout the country in perpetual slight motion in the ever-moving air, and by the conjured labours of millions of pores the substance of whole forests of solid wood is slowly extracted from the fleeting winds. Every year it rains heavily, it rains leaves, these leaves woven from the winds. Why is there not a moutainous result quite soon where there are woods? This question may be stupid, but I do not find that the answers I have ever received are very good.

Another thing. Why do we not notice a great change of air in the summer from what it was in the winter? There are those leaves extracting that vast amount of gas from the air, a process not active in winter, and yet we do not seem to suffer from it, do not notice any difference. Again, this question may seem too obviously the mark of an uninstructed mind; but I am relieved to find that Mr H E Bates says that this very thing does affect him personally. 'It is as though – perhaps actually because – the air has been sucked up by a million leaves.' And he goes on to say (in *Through The Wood*), 'W H Hudson himself noticed this and had some comments on it in relation to the New Forest, where he felt that the great expanse of trees seemed to suck up all life and leave the mind and body and spirit as flabby as a sponge.

He pointed out how pale the Hampshire people of that district looked, as though they were literally robbed of air.'

But one does not raise such questions with much hope of replies from specialists. They are far better at naming things than in answering questions of interest. If they can name a problem they often think they have solved it. 'Perhaps nothing is more curious in the history of the human mind,' said Ruskin, 'than the way in which the science of botany has become oppressed with nomenclature.' Thus do they overcome the problems of reality by simply labelling reality, just as in other departments the significance of a man's point of view, his truth in which he passionately believes, is side-stepped by a label – his truth becoming merely an -ism. Still, I do not worry myself about getting answers to my question. I rather like not getting them. And I can truthfully say that the phenomenon itself is good enough for me. Gazing upon phenomena, I find that my problems are not solved; but they are dissolved.

And of all phenomena concerning trees, that which appeals to me most is – the trunk. For me the most beautiful sight in the woods is not the foliage, not the flowers, not the squirrel, not the deer – it is the trunks of trees of about thirty years old upwards. Especially the ash: the smooth grey bark; then a patch of dark moss; above it a patch of pale-green lichen in beautiful filigree pressed against the bark; then a number of white spots; then bark again; then moss again – no pattern, yet all pattern, no design yet all design, making a rounded tapestry beyond all the powers of art to render. No bright colours yet many colours – and in winter-time how often we see from the train window, tree-trunks almost as green as grass set in the gloom of the leafless boughs, taking the rain and the dusk in silent alertness. Once having been given four freshly cut logs of silver birch, I did not burn them (in any case they wouldn't have been good as fire), but put them on a shelf as pictures. And I assure you they held my attention for many a day. Often I have been glad that I am not a painter; never more so than when confronted by some magnificent tree-trunk. Here is something that cannot be told, cannot be rendered. Here is the object, the thing itself, so staggering in its presence that we fall back from it, the intricacy of the totality cannot be copied, and it is the intricacy that is the picture; before it the art of suggestion is powerless, only the lower art of photography can give the total sum of the minutiae. Look at that old silver-birch trunk: knuckled, notched, and dented with its ditches, ruts, and causeways, all subservient to the majesty of design; look at the splashes of smooth white irregularly placed, the bark itself, not lichen: if a house-painter did a post with dabs of white here and there like that we would think it a poor, strange piece of work: but here it is magnificent, the impression of the Whole is terrific – we must leave our pen, our brush in face of it, abandon art as a hopeless substitute. Look at that old Scotch pine tree. It has no lichen, all the beauty is in the bark alone: rubbed, fluted, seamed, deeply chiselled, it is a personality, it is a Being. Perhaps that's what I'm after here in these fumbling words: the power and the glory here is in the *substance* of the thing, and art is without substance.

Truly trees are Beings. We feel that to be so. Hence their silence, their indifference to us is almost exasperating. We would speak to them, we would ask their message; for they seem to hold some weighty truth, some special secret – and though sometimes we receive their blessing, they do not answer, they make no sign. When we look upon a man we find that he is not satisfied, he wishes he were something else, or had done something else. When we look upon a monkey we see that clearly it is a lost soul. When we look upon a sheep we see that it is unhappy in itself. When we look upon a cow we cannot be certain that underneath its apparent calm it is not concealing a great unease. Whitman said that he could turn and live with the animals. I would not join him. But many men have turned and lived with trees. They are much more companionable than cows. Thoreau would sometimes refuse to make an engagement with a friend on the ground that he had 'an appointment with a tree'. What then is their final appeal, their message to mankind? Isaac Rosenberg alone has told it.

> Then spake I to the tree,
> Were ye your own desire
> What is it ye would be?
> Answered the tree to me,
> I am my own desire;
> I am what I would be.

22 Firewood

While carrying out my business of thinning the wood I piled up the thick poles which I had cut down, in batches of a hundred – for, working by the piece, I made so much per lug and so much per hundred poles. These piles of poles made a very satisfactory sight for me, since they were carried away at intervals to be used as firewood in the neighbouring village, superb firewood at that. It gave me considerable pleasure to know that one result of my work up here was that I supplied wood for a whole village throughout the winter. At irregular periods it was carted away by Reggie and the boys. I would hear his high voice from a long way off, shouting at the horse, and about half an hour later they would arrive with the trailer which they used for loading up.

One of the reasons why I am especially attracted by ash is because it has so much fire in it. That may not be the proper way to put it; but it certainly seems as if flame resides inside the wood. When we have *put fire* to wood, what do we see? We do not see the fire *devouring* the wood as it goes along: we see the wood *becoming fire*, 'bursting into flames' as we say. Everything has fire in it, we are told, even stones – though it takes much extra heat to set a stone on fire. Of all the receptacles of fire in the world, wood is the most famous and our debt to it without measure. It is easy to understand how the ancient Aryans regarded trees as the *storerooms* of heat and that the sun itself was periodically recruited from the fire which resided in the sacred oak.

And of all trees, Ash becomes fire best. It need not be seasoned first, it burns almost equally well whether dry or cut down yesterday. If you cut down a bundle of fresh, green ash-twigs they do perfectly for lighting your fire, they are ready-made crackers, they are children's fireworks. Try the same thing with hazel and you'll never get your fire lit at all. Whenever I go to any new place in the country I look round at once to see if there are any ash woods nearby, for if so I know that I need not depend upon dry twigs for lighting fires. To my amazement I found many woodmen ignorant of this, while one or two who were not ignorant of it gave me surprising examples of wasteful folly caused by such ignorance. Observing the old man who worked with Reggie and the boys, taking home some hazel-faggots for his fire when there were heaps of ash around, I asked him why. He simply said that he had always done so. The fact that he had always done so was advanced in terms of a scientific statement that hazel made as good faggots as ash.

I used to take home a pole every day from the wood, and thus I was always in command of a magnificent fire – costing nothing save the labour of carriage. Then the bitter cold of a winter's evening was transformed by the white-hot wood and I was nearly as happy in front of this earthly flame as in the summer under the sun.

I need not say that this job stimulated my interest in the financial aspect of fire-logs. All of us here were paid as woodmen, so much a week, or so much the piece; but occasionally I became familiar with the other sort of woodmen who, working on their own, made a good

deal more by simply extracting wood and selling it –
without any interest in the plantations. They made more,
but of course they had to work hard for it, and to take
risks. The man who really makes big profits is the man
at the far end who distributes it – the man who neither
plants, thins, tends, or extracts the wood. When I learnt
the surprising prices charged for a sack of logs in the
neighbouring towns, I realized that if you want to get
rich in modern society you should not aim at securing
the Means of Production, but rather the Means of Distribution. For today it is written – Blessed is he who
distributes.

23 Winter Scenes; The Calamity

I looked forward during the day to my superb evening
fires in the winter months. It is not often very cold in a
wood even when it is biting outside, in fact the difference
in temperature on the same day in the wood as against
the field, is sometimes phenomenal. Nevertheless there
were spells when my hands were too cold to grip the
axe and the wind so keen that no amount of work served
to make me warm. At such times I wanted to get away
from the wood – though not into any other agricultural
job.

Often it was merely damp, windless, and dreary. At
such times I felt curiously lonely amongst the trees, in
a pleasantly sad sort of way. The silence was so melancholy, the mystery of the trees and the dark undergrowth
so great, that I felt exiled from truth as well as from

mankind. I used to grope my way in explorations into the deeper darkness beyond my immediate position, peering round with something of the expectancy and the fear of a man in a haunted house.

I frequently came upon fresh samples of fallen trunks lying on the ground in various stages of decomposition: there were some great hulks whose outer crust was as soft as earth, and whose inner caverns, on being exposed by the bill-hook, revealed curious insects curled up here and there in holes evidently intended as dormitories for the winter. That was one type, but there was another I almost preferred – the long trunk, sunk low, covered with moss and leafage, becoming indistinguishable from the ground as it tapered to what was once its top. I had one favourite of this kind. It was considerably long: the thickest end was like a mound, and it gradually tapered on getting smaller and smaller until it became level with the ground, and only the freshness of the moss showed me where the 'wood' was. And if I walked along upon this strange rise, it was exactly as if I were walking upon something as soft as a mountain swamp.

The moss was deep and clear upon these barks. It was also laid across the whole floor of the wood. In the winter one becomes conscious of this new glory. When the spring flowers are long forgotten and the new series is in hidden preparation out of sight and of thought; when the bracken that rose so high and green has browned and fallen down; when the herb-willow has posted its final envelope of seed; when the latest storm has removed the last leaves from tree and bush; when the long, low kingdom of dog's mercury has disappeared – then the ground is not bare, it is not desolate: it shines again with a new growth; we enter the reign of moss. This is one of the sweetest and dearest of all plants. We think of it in the mass and speak of winding mossy ways, as so we should; but if we look close we see that it is a network of the most delicate little fronds whose massed formations give us the soft, deep carpet. It is not seen during the summer, and where we do discern it, it is parched and poor; but in the chill of winter when all other life is in abeyance this is in the ascendant, the floor of the earth is cushioned and all the scars of mortality are bandaged and made blessed.

During the short winter days I sometimes arrived in the wood while the moon was still the only light, and day had not yet broken in. At this hour, before the particular beam of the sun had changed the scene, the atmosphere was expectant. Nature appeared to be listening carefully for something and was evidently awaiting some great event. I did not dare say a word, even to cough. Objects which in the light of day were animated only with the life of plants, became informed with the life of beasts, so that mere bushes looked like tigers about to spring. When the day broke in at last it did not do so slowly as it is supposed to do in these climes, there came a moment when the darkness began to lighten up quite steadily and swiftly. The moon started to go out as if someone were turning down a lamp rather gingerly, and the light of the hidden sun illuminated the scene almost at the rate of theatrical lights slowly bathing a stage that had been in darkness. At other times, arriving on a misty morning, I found that the wood was of immense size, receding into the distance on all sides as if it were boundless in space and belonging to any Age. The boles of the trees, erect in the mist, were as thin and pale as the pencillings in a Chinese drawing. They had no strength or substance: it would have been easy to rub them all out of the picture. As the day advanced and the sun rose to cancel the morning mist, the scene shifted. The Present Day came back again, the wood occupied a given number of acres, the trees were hard and firm once more. Then the afternoon sun was turned upon them, and they held the light, they stopped it and took it upon themselves, each a shining post, while the wind blew and the strange, unhappy hours passed by – for even in a wood at this time of the day, more so in a wood than elsewhere when the wind blows unceasingly, all solitary men are perplexed and feel the motion of infelicity.

These were days when a hot drink was the very thing in the course of the morning, and I never forgot to bring out my thermos-flask. Its cap was broken, lacking which I generally brought a china cup with me. But sometimes I forgot this item. However, I had a remedy when this happened. At this time of the year many more varieties of fungi attracted my attention. There was one species which particularly appealed to me. It was pale yellow and shaped like a large wine-glass. On the occasions when I forgot to bring out my cup I simply plucked one of these stalked cups made of fungus, filled it from my thermos-flask, and thus had my drink in comfort.

It was not possible to do much work in the intense cold nor in heavy rain. When it rained slightly it was quite all right, and many a time when I should have had to seek shelter if in the fields, I could carry on in the wood without a raincoat. But a continuously wet day made it impossible (especially earlier in the year when the leaves were still on the trees, for then your stroke brought down a great deal of extra water upon you) for the axe then became too slippery to hold. When it snowed my work stopped immediately, of course. I have often referred here to the silences peculiar to the woodman's life; but is there any silence so deep and rare as that bestowed by snow? Whether in a wood, or outside, it is a wonderful thing in our machine age to find the world in the morning ankle-deep in snow. Then the unwonted silence that falls upon our life is truly magnificent; and when the snow has been really heavy making all lanes and many roads impassable, the sense of isolation in our silence carries us right back to the days when communication even between villages was scarce and chequered. One heavy fall of snow in the country, and modern civilization is *silenced*!

These winter scenes are related in my mind with another scene, more human and more sad. Reggie occasionally came across from his part of the estate to see me. I think of a certain Friday when I heard him call my name (he used my Christian name), and appeared coming through the trees with his dog and his gun, which he often carried. He had some agricultural extra clothing-coupons to give me, and brought a paper for me to sign. And we fell into conversation about this and that, his early life in Devon, the present life here, the wages young boys got nowadays and what they did with the money, his rank of Corporal in the Home Guard, and so on. He draped himself against a tree as usual, his remarkable flaxen hair, his brown face, and workman's clothes fitting into the surroundings perfectly and, indeed, beautifully. Thus we stood and talked upon the general affairs of life, amongst the friendly trees, well cornered from the rough traffic of the world, far away from the great battles that were then being fought, insensible in this leafy harbour to the noise and rumour of the field, secure from calamity and the sudden dart of death, or so it seemed. Presently he went away. He called to his little genteel black dog, and disappeared through the trees out of my sight, and went across a field towards the scene of his death. For he was never to return along these ways nor would that voice be heard in the woods any more. Later in the afternoon there was a dreadful explosion, louder and more earth-shaking than others I had heard in the neighbourhood, due to the practising soldiery. This explosion was not made by the army. Reggie had picked up a bomb which he imagined was quite harmless. He had brought it back to his shed. He thought it was a smoke-bomb of some sort and decided to examine its interior. Finding it difficult to dismantle, he took a hammer and began to tap it. The boys, who were standing near, became frightened and tried to dissuade him; but he sat there bending over the bomb, tapping at it. It exploded, blowing his hands off and killing him – the boys escaping death, but not injury.

The whole village shuddered at this meaningless tragedy. The catastrophe of our time was focused upon the body of this one man, cut down suddenly in the midst of abounding life.

24 Farewell to the Wood

In the company of flowers we know happiness. In the company of trees we are able to *think*, they foster meditation. Trees are very intellectual. There is nowhere on earth we can think so well as in a thin wood resting against a tree. Such at least is my experience, and it is the ultimate memory that I shall carry away from this place. For in parting I know that the greatest wrench of all is in connection with the old oak tree (under which or in the vicinity of which I have written this account). It is not easy to say farewell to it; not easy to pass from the best spot in the whole world between the hours of eight and ten in the morning during May and August. For as I have said, that is the time when the sun rested upon my seat.

Sometimes I could wish that my love of the sun were less genuine. How often I have felt compelled to alter my plans for the day's work because the sun unexpectedly came out to shine against my special tree or on some other favourite spot! I have been about to do a portion of thinning marked out as the minimum for the morning, when, the sun coming out, I have abandoned my schedule in order to seize, if only for a few cloud-chequered intervals, the gift of the sun at that hour, in that blessed place. I have had to turn back for the same reason, while on my way into the neighbouring town to get some much-needed things. The sun deflects me from my courses. I mention this as the kind of psychological fact that holds a certain interest, since we scarcely allow enough for the part such things play in the destinies of men. I often wonder at anyone accepting the Materialistic Conception of History. Many people, after Marx, began to say that circumstances are the cause of any given life. But since circumstances can be inside one as well as outside, the dictum holds little absolute meaning. Put two men in front of me, equal in talent, similar in circumstance, one loving, the other indifferent to the sun, and I will roughly outline their careers. The man who really loved the sun would miss vital appointments, fumble momentous opportunities: the other would forge ahead. No self-made rich industrialist has ever loved the sun. Such a man may well benefit mankind, it is not to be denied. But also, that other man, in receiving into himself that warmth and that light, may perchance give back something to his fellows, tell something of what he has felt, what he has *known*, illuminate the darkness of the exiled, even raise up the parched and withering hearts of men. Let me then take a knife and inscribe upon the ancient oak these words – INDECISIVE, FOOLISH, SELFISH, LAZY: A MAN MAY BE ALL THAT AND WORSE, AND YET BE A BENEFACTOR OF THE WORLD, IF HE BUT LOVE TO SIT IN THE SUN LEANING AGAINST A TREE!

Having inscribed those words, I must take my leave. I shall return to this spot. It will remain the same tomorrow as today. When I return I will step back in time. I will step out of time. For one of the things that has struck me most about this wood, or of any sequestered wood known to me, is that having turned off from your road and entered the wood, you have really gone through a *gate* which now is closed behind you, and your ordinary world is shut out with all its noise and sorrow and care. Once inside, you seem to have stepped out of the flow of civilized time and to have entered into the peace of the ever-juvenile eternities of earth. The road along which you have come may be in a lonely rural retreat; but it belongs to your century and as you go along it you are in the atmosphere of that century. You enter the wood – and you might just as well be in the Middle Ages. When I hear people speak of the Dark Ages, I remind myself how in those days the sun shone in just the same way as it does now, and the flowers glittered in woods where there was no difference from what we see today. Outside we think our way back into the past, trying to picture the village then, the lie of the land, the agricultural equipment. Inside the wood we are in the past as well as in the present. Perhaps the time will come when people will speak of these days as the Black Ages or the Darker Ages; if so let them then turn and read my words here and remember that the sun shone upon us even as upon them, that the trees looked the same in the glory of his light, and that at this time also you could side-step into happiness and peace.

Thus I attempt to say farewell, as I look around at this secluded scene. I look across at my sun-dial, wondering if that will be still there when I come again. For in the actual prosaic matter of knowing the hour of day I had no watch and worked outside the whole clock-world and dwelt far from the frame of mind of the BBC announcer who says 'It is just coming up to half a minute to eight.' But I did not quite dispense with a clock. I used the lofty, golden time-piece of the sun and a tree which cast a clear, clean shadow with its trunk. At exactly twelve o'clock I stuck a stick in the shadow-line. Thus I always knew when it was twelve so long as the clock was unclouded. I put in other sticks for other hours, and so could tell the time of day within half an hour.

I look across at the growing and maturing trees now free from all entanglements. I had come to a wild entanglement, and now, as far as I can see in any direction, a free plantation meets my eye, accomplished by the labour of my hands alone. Nothing that I have ever done has given me more satisfaction than this, nor shall I hope to find again so great a happiness. Realizing something of what the work meant to me, and perhaps truthfully saying that he was very pleased with the result, Rolf entered this area of about twelve acres, in the books of the Estate, as COLLIS PIECE, and by that name it is now known. Thus then do I achieve what had never occurred to me could conceivably happen, that a piece of English earth and forest would carry my name into the future. Nobody is ever likely to confer upon me Honours or Titles or City Freedoms, nor will any Monument be raised to perpetuate and repeat my name. But this plot of earth will do it, these trees will do it: in the summer they will glitter and shine for me, and in the winter, mourn.